Beth,
Please share these
stories - God Bless
America -

My Father's War

Memories from Our Honored WWII Soldiers

Charley Valera 1-13-17

Charley Valera

MY FATHER'S WAR
MEMORIES FROM OUR HONORED WWII SOLDIERS

iUniverse books may be ordered through booksellers or by contacting:

iUniverse
1663 Liberty Drive
Bloomington, IN 47403
www.iuniverse.com
1-800-Authors (1-800-288-4677)

ISBN: 978-1-5320-0952-5 (sc)
ISBN: 978-1-5320-0953-2 (hc)
ISBN: 978-1-5320-0951-8 (e)

Library of Congress Control Number: 2016919088

Print information available on the last page.

iUniverse rev. date: 12/14/2016

To my late father, Giovanni "Gene" Valera, and my late
mother, Celia Cali. She had the endurance and patience
to raise us as loving and forever proud children.

Thanks to my big brothers, John, Joseph, and Sebastian. Now maybe
we know the Old Man a bit better. Thank you to my two great
sons, Anthony and Andrew, and my wonderful wife, Cheryl, for her
help, patience, and support of this long but worthwhile project.

God bless America.

CONTENTS

You'll finally hear their stories!

They returned home—not just my father but your father as well. This book is about all our fathers and their families.

These veterans are finally telling their World War II stories. This book is about their war and how it changed their lives—and ours—forever. From small towns in central Massachusetts, these young men gave up their early years, and some their lives, for the very freedom we take for granted today.

Before you is a testament by our fellow neighbors who gave so much, endured unbelievable conditions, fought battle-toughened enemies, and came home after a brutal world war, hoping for some normalcy and to raise us as their children and grandchildren. You'll fight beside them and laugh at their stories and sometimes-crazy antics.

In this fantastic book, you'll hear and read their own words as they fought for our freedom during World War II as young men. Alongside these incredible stories are a host of our neighbors' original photographs and letters, most of which have never been seen in public before. Some are disturbing, and some are awe inspiring beyond our everyday comprehension. These stories have been locked up with these wonderful Americans for more than seventy years.

Love, war, family, and religion are all rolled into the stories of each and every soldier you'll meet. Join us on a journey from thirty thousand feet in a B-17 over Germany to liberating the Nazi concentration camp at Buchenwald to dive-bombing the Japanese Imperial Army, missing your sweetheart, eating bad food, and eating great food with a bottle of scotch.

Sure, they fought for us, but let's be real: in the trenches and foxholes, they did what was necessary mostly for one another. They were soldiers in arms fighting to protect one another's futures.

Additional personal photos and the interviews on video of these brave men can be found at www.charleyvalera.com.

FOREWORD

Every once in a while, a project not of my own making comes along, and I just have to jump in and do whatever I must to be involved. Charley Valera's collection of amazing stories, *My Father's War: Memories from Our Honored WWII Soldiers*, is one such project.

Charley contacted me for some advice, one thing led to the next, and soon I was knee-deep in the project. As a veteran of Operation Desert Storm (army), I am obviously drawn to military stories. This book, however, has proven to be much more than that. It's a living history lesson, generously passed down by men (and women) who, in moments of selfless courage, defined their generation as the greatest our country has ever known. Together they fought evil—in its purest form—and were relentless in their pursuit of ridding the world of unprecedented barbarism.

My Father's War: Memories from Our Honored WWII Soldiers is an incredible collection of eyewitness testimonies from WWII veterans: pilots and crew members who honed their lethal skills in life-and-death missions they flew every day. It's about soldiers and sailors who beat back the bile in their throats to do their duties and complete their dangerous missions. And all of them—to this very day—still refuse to make any fuss over their accomplishments. Most just say, "I was only doing my job."

Although I believe the United States of America is still the greatest country on earth, it is not without its flaws. We have, unfortunately, evolved from a "we" society to a "me" society; many folks are less compelled to help others unless there's something in it for them.

This book is a stark reminder of the greatness that we come from. It offers the true definitions—by example—of patriotism, sacrifice, and bravery. The veterans of WWII stood up and did what was needed to protect the weak from the strong, even when they were scared or tired of fighting. Regardless of the task set before them, they gave more than they took and, in doing so, built extraordinary lives—as you'll experience in each story.

While serving a purpose higher than themselves, the men and women within this collection of stories built America into the superpower it is today. We need to remember that. We need to honor that. We need to honor them.

I'd like to thank my friend Charley Valera for allowing me to take the passenger seat on this wonderful journey. With each page turned, I have been humbled and brought to an even deeper appreciation for all I have. Without our WWII veterans, we—yes, all of us—would not enjoy the lives we live today.

Steve Manchester, Gulf War veteran and best-selling author of *The Rockin' Chair*

CAST OF CHARACTERS

Book 1
Captain Vincent "Bill" Purple

Book 2
Corporal Fernand E. Frechette

Book 3
First Lieutenant Thomas J. and Elaine McDonald

Book 4
Private First Class George J. Pelletier

Book 5
Tech Corporal Charles M. Sanderson

Book 6
Staff Sergeant Albert George Pinard

Book 7
Staff Sergeant Santo DiSalvo

Book 8
Tech Sergeant Joseph R. Chiminiello

Book 9
Second Lieutenant Charles R. Rogers

Book 10
Staff Sergeant Lauri K. Rautio

Book 11
Very Honorable Mentions
John Casey, Walt Cutting, Mario Lanza, Erwin G. Markowitz,
Anthony Hmura, Raphael Godin, Frederick L. Cuddy

PREFACE

Life is similar to a hallway—a beautiful hallway of ornate railings and oak, with the finest crown moldings you can imagine, an endless hallway of beautiful doors, each one different. One might evoke feelings for your family, another might entice you to a warm vacation, and yet another might have jingle bells hanging over the doorknob. There are countless doors, and you can't see to the end of the beautiful winding hallway. But we each see our own individual hallway, filled with doors of opportunity and happiness. Most of them, anyhow ...

However, we've all opened doors we wished we hadn't; some we can't seem to close fast enough. But like secrets, once you cross through them, they are forever a piece of you—like it or not. The doors we choose make us different people as we open them and walk through. Personally, I love doors and can't wait to see what's on the other side of each one.

We're pushed through some doors, forced through by outside influences, knowing that once the doorknob has been turned, our lives will be instantly changed. I'm not talking about your first time on the Internet or your first lesson as a student pilot. I'm talking about war! World War II is this book's soup du jour. Nations made up of ten, twenty, fifty, and more million people together changed not only their own lives but the life of every person born since then—the baby boomers and their children.

Building a military of the might and magnitude needed during a world war is incredible. It's like directing an ocean of fish to swim at a particular time in a particular direction for a particular length of time: all of them, at three o'clock tomorrow, will swim clockwise for one hour. If it sounds far-fetched, imagine almost every person on the planet bearing arms, in one way or another, against another group—which is aiming its weapons right back.

One—just one—bombing raid had more than fifteen hundred aircraft in formation. Each plane held ten or more men, expecting the worst. A line made of that many aircraft would stretch across the sky for two hundred miles. Each plane was loaded with devastating bombs to be dropped as precisely as possible on its targets. These were barely tested aircraft flown by kids in their early twenties, with a bare minimum of flight training and experience. Most had never left home before, let alone gone to a hostile country—or driven a car, or shot a gun, or thought they'd ever amount to much. They probably hadn't given it much thought either.

The stories you're about to read are firsthand accounts of some Massachusetts World War II veterans whom I've had the honor to meet and interview. Here is the story of how young, ordinary people from modest backgrounds became incredible soldiers, fighting a nasty, close battle that ranged from dropping bombs on barely visible targets to hand-to-hand combat—even fistfights. Perhaps some of the stories aren't exactly how events transpired, but they do capture exactly how each person remembers them.

Fast-forward seventy years or so. I have my pilot's license. I'd decided to pursue flying for some unknown reason—because of forces of nature out of my control. A magnificent door was opened that changed my life and presented me with new and exciting opportunities.

In 2011, a group of pilots I fly with—known as the Fitchburg Pilots Association—were giving free plane rides to kids during one of our Young Eagles events. This is something we do twice a year in the hope of creating a new generation of pilots, as well as creating a fun and memorable experience for the kids, their parents, and us—the pilots. I know, I know—how nice. But on this one day, on this one flight, one kid opened a new door with his grandfather. I didn't know the old man, who was white-haired and hunched over in a white T-shirt, or his grandson, who appeared to be your average-looking twelve-year-old.

They happened to go to the airport diner for breakfast on that sunny Saturday morning. When they saw we were offering free rides, grandpa asked grandson if he wanted to go—they would fly together, along with one of our pilots. How could the boy resist?

I was randomly selected to fly them. As we were walking to my Cessna Skyhawk, grandpa told me that he used to fly during the war and that he'd been a turret gunner. *Wow!* Me being me, I jokingly asked if he wanted me to remove the backseat for him so he could be more comfortable sitting on the floor. He laughed and said, "No thanks."

To me, it was just another fun flight, showing off the beauty of flying and the scenery of central Massachusetts in early summer. But a few days later, I received a call at the flight school I own from a woman asking me if I might know who had flown her son and her father-in-law that day. She wanted some photos, if there were any. At the time, I was the president of the Fitchburg Pilots Association, so I would field calls and coordinate this type of event. I remembered the flight and replied that not only did I have photos, but a local cable station had captured it on video as well.

She explained that the flight had opened up a dialogue between grandpa and grandson. They had talked about his war service, what he had done and when, and how it had affected him. I was honored to know that I had had a small hand in opening those doors. The boy's mom and dad were in awe. They had never known about the grandfather's war service. Many veterans of WWII—including him—had come home and never discussed the war ever again, closing the door almost completely. They wanted to put the experience behind them and get their lives back to some sense of normalcy. They became busy, raising families, getting jobs, and making new friends, knowing they could never make up for the years lost during the war.

Besides, who would want to go into that room again anyhow? Who would want to hear about that old stuff? We do! The children, the grandchildren, and their children—and that's who this book is for.

I have links to video clips and additional photos of the actual veterans, bringing to life the people you're going to read about. You'll be able to see them and hear them say some of the words that you'll be reading here. I'm willing to bet you're not too far removed from one of these amazing men—maybe a cousin, uncle, or grandfather.

As I write their stories, many of these veterans are now ninety to ninety-six years old. We should all salute these brave men and be sincerely grateful for the sacrifices they made for our country and for each one of us.

Charley Valera

ACKNOWLEDGMENTS

How do I thank everyone? First and foremost, I am grateful to my best friend and wife, Cheryl, for encouraging me to push on even when it was raining and snowing. Thank you to the many friends and fellow WWII baby boomers who also encouraged me to fight the fight and keep things moving along in anticipation of reading these chapters. Also, with enormous gratitude to all the veterans who dug deep once more to share stories they've tried most of their lives to forget so they could move on in life. Some additional gratitude to special helpers, such as best-selling author Steve Manchester, my editor and friend, for so much help and encouragement as he read this.

Thank you to Stacey Alcorn, she knows more people than I do and is always willing to share. Another big help came from Mark Bondanza, attorney, author, and friend, who is always willing to offer encouragement and advice whenever I ask. A huge thank you Jim Powell, my chief pilot and friend, for covering for me at the FCA Flight Center while I was writing instead of managing. Last but certainly not least, thank you to all the families that reached out to me about their own father's war efforts and wanted their stories told, and so many others.

I guess it's fair to say we can all thank each other for pulling these historic stories together. Thank you for your time, effort, and service.

Courage—Mental or moral strength to venture, persevere, and withstand danger, fear, or difficulty. The ability to do something that you know is difficult or dangerous.

Hero—A man admired for his achievements and noble qualities. One who shows great courage.

Valor—Strength of mind or spirit that enables a person to encounter danger with firmness, personal bravery.

—Merriam-Webster dictionary

United States of America 1941–1945. Freedom from fear and want. Freedom of speech and religion.

—Stamped on the World War II Victory Medal

INTRODUCTION

We all know someone who was there, in World War II—probably a close relative, such as a father, brother, uncle, or grandparents. Most of us have hardly heard their stories about their young war years. We may have been afraid to ask about their stories, and they may assume we don't want to know. But this was such an important life changer, with certain death and torture on the line every day—waking up every morning for days and years without their families close by, constant battles going on, and amazing destruction. It was for us they fought, so we should know their stories. We should honor them by chronicling their amazing, heroic war efforts before they are gone and it's too late.

My dad was a member of the Eighth Army Air Force 329th Ninety-Third Bombardment Group (Heavy) and served from January 14, 1942, through November 23, 1945. His engagements, according to his DD-214 official military discharge papers, included the Rhineland, Ardennes, northern France, Normandy, Egypt, Libya, Tunisia, Sicily, the Po Valley, Rome, Arno, and Central Europe.

But he hardly had a story to tell.

My dad, Giovanni (John) "Gene" Valera, was clearly my inspiration for this research. He was born May 19, 1919, and died peacefully on October 17, 1999. Although he was our father, we had to put pieces together to know the real man. We knew his parents emigrated from a remote area in Pietraperzia, Sicily. His father, Cologero (my namesake), had died when Dad was only seven years old, paving the way for he and his five brothers and one sister to support their family during those difficult depression years. Being a single parent, his mom barely spoke the language as she raised a family between world wars.

One common rare story they shared was how some of the boys would go blueberry picking before school and sell the berries after school to raise money. But not much more than that story was shared.

Dad was a 1935 graduate of Saint Bernard's High School in Fitchburg, Massachusetts, where he was a star athlete in track, football, and basketball. In 1985, he and his high school basketball team were inducted into the Basketball Hall of Fame in Springfield, Massachusetts, during a ceremony hosted by NBA Commissioner Larry O'Brien.

But I believe the war changed him dramatically. He went from an athletic, outgoing young man to being more withdrawn and quiet. Asking him about his activities or whereabouts was out of the question. He returned from the war a very private man who showed little emotion. However, he was never too far away.

After the war, he went to work at General Electric in Fitchburg, and he retired from there in 1985. My three brothers and I knew Dad had it tough—we could tell. He *was* tough. The early sacrifices he made growing up shaped his life, our lives, and the lives of our children. As for the war, all he said was that he was a cook and spent thirteen months in England—no more, no less.

A few years ago, one of my nephews, John Valera (John is the English version of Giovanni), was asking me about my dad's war efforts. Sadly, my siblings and I knew virtually nothing. I have only three war photos with my dad in them. So John and I obtained rough copies of my father's DD-214 discharge papers. That's when we saw, for the first time, his eleven campaigns and where he was for almost three years— two years, nine months, and fourteen days overseas to be exact. He was twenty-two years old and would be US property for the next 1,409 days of a war with US involvement lasting approximately 1,364 days. Corporal Giovanni Valera was honorably discharged from the United States Army, Eighth Army Air Force, 329th Bombardment Group (H), Ninety-Third Bomb Group on November 23, 1945.

My father knew my mother before the war. Celia Cali was one of six children from Sebastiano and Maria Cali, also Sicilian immigrants. Gene and Celia were married in June 1946 and had three boys and a girl. However, the little girl, the baby of the family, died unexpectedly in 1956. As a result, the Valeras decided to have another child: me. I was born in 1957.

He was Dad to us. He gave no birthday gifts or Christmas presents. He insisted he didn't want any, either, although he never refused my pan of sauce or a fresh ricotta pie. Holidays were a bother and interrupted his private routine. But he was Dad. He opened many doors during his war years, and I'm willing to bet he wished he didn't have to. But they all did. They enlisted together and fought together, and some died together, leaving those going home to carry the burden and deal with the deaths of many family members and friends.

We should all be very proud of their efforts, even though we may not have asked and they may not have told us. Once again, they protected us with their silence. I was allowed inside for brief moments. Here are their stories.

GIOVANNI "GENE" VALERA
U.S. ARMY 8ᵀᴴ AIR FORCE
329ᵀᴴ NINETY-THIRD BOMBARDMENT GROUP (HEAVY)

Book 1

CAPTAIN VINCENT "BILL" PURPLE

Chapter 1

If You Didn't Get Hurt,
It Was the Greatest Experience
You Could Ever Have

Vincent "Bill" Piepol, changed in 1951 to Purple, was born May 7, 1924, in Athol, Massachusetts. More than ninety years later, he lives in the next town over, called Petersham. He is a widower and has two grown children, Cynthia and Phillip.

Back when Purple was born, people traveled in Athol by horse or in a limited number of automobiles. Back in the 1920s and 1930s, it was fun, simple, and easy living for a kid; you just had to do your chores and be a respectful part of the family.

Purple's parents were immigrants from Poland; his mom came over in 1906 and his dad in 1904. For reasons unbeknownst to Purple, they settled in Athol. His parents became lawful citizens of the United States and brought six American children into the world. Purple went to Athol High School and graduated in the spring of 1941. What timing.

On December 7, 1941, Purple was driving with a friend when they heard on the radio that the Japanese had just bombed Pearl Harbor. They didn't even know where Pearl Harbor was. Purple and his friends didn't have any real knowledge of world politics. "Didn't need to," he told me seventy years later. "It didn't matter to us at that time of our lives." Although they were not fully aware of the battles and the details of what was going on in Europe, doors would soon appear for Purple that he couldn't have imagined in his wildest dreams.

In the summer of 1942, Purple had a friend who had joined the US Army aviation unit. "But he didn't make the cut," explained Purple. Making "the cut" was a tough challenge. At that point, the army had been using civilian flight training programs. Basic flight maneuvers were discussed and taught, but most of the recruits at that time didn't have what the instructors would consider competent enough piloting skills to continue their flight training. But his friend did share with Purple what flying was like—how free and alive he felt and how challenging it was just to learn the basics. They discussed the process of learning to fly, and he explained to Purple what would be needed to pass the rigorous Aviation Cadet Testing Program. Until then, Purple was yet to fly in an aircraft.

In July 1942, Purple visited the airport in nearby Orange, Massachusetts, where he enthusiastically took his first airplane ride. It was a two-seat Piper Cub, a pretty yellow plane with front and back seating. Doors opened upward; it was a slow-flying, easy aircraft to fly. There was a New England breeze that day, and the view flying right over the Quabbin Reservoir was fantastic. Life was looking up for Purple. "Had an airplane ride. It didn't scare me and I didn't get sick, so I figured I'd try aviation," he said with a chuckle, "and join the air corps."

From that very moment, from that one ride, Purple decided he would join the US Army Air Force (known as the United States Army Air Corps until June 20, 1941).

After graduating from Athol High School, Purple wanted to sign up for the armed services. But he was only seventeen years old. "I needed permission from my parents to join and fight the war," he said with a grin. His mother finally agreed to allow him to join the air force, so in 1942, he applied for the Aviation Cadet Testing Program. By joining, he would avoid the inevitable draft and choose his role in the war effort.

Chapter 2

From Citizen to Soldier

In 1940, the United States imposed a Selective Service, or draft, where men between the ages of twenty-one and thirty-six were required to register for military services. Although this was still peacetime for the United States, the rest of the world was in turmoil, causing our leaders to look forward. Everyone who registered had a number; when it was drawn, your number was up and you were drafted. During the first year of the draft, more than 50 percent were ineligible for the draft because of health reasons or illiteracy; more than 20 percent were illiterate.

As we all know, on December 7, 1941, Japan attacked the United States at Pearl Harbor and we were now officially in World War II. By 1942, we were at war and there were some major policy changes in the draft; ages were now between eighteen and thirty-seven. As the war progressed, so did the draft. It permitted blacks to be included in 1943—to around 10 percent. In all, more than 50 million American men were registered for the draft, and more than 16 million actually served in the military. In total, there would be estimates of 1.9 billion people serving in the war with more than 72 million casualties—simply staggering numbers.[1]

Troops were being drafted and everyone was lining up everywhere to join a branch of the military. "I was ordered to report to Springfield,

---

1 http://www.wwiifoundation.org/students/wwii-facts-figures/ March 2015.

Massachusetts, in January 1943 with three other friends," reported Purple. "Dad said 'hi' and 'bye,' and we went to the post office and that was it." Long, drawn-out good-byes were yet to be invented.

Once in Springfield, the recruits were transported toward becoming soldiers. "We were in trains and shipped like cargo from Springfield to Buffalo to Columbus, Ohio, and on to Atlantic City. It was a long roundabout train ride just to get us to basic training," Purple said. No doubt, the ride had them all wondering what they were getting themselves into. "When we finally stopped, we were all starved from being in a train for eighteen hours. They gave all the guys chili." It was an easy meal to make and to feed to a cargo train full of young men—a taste of what was to come. Other than skiing trips as a kid, this was the first time Purple had really been away from home.

Initial military training for Purple was held right on the New Jersey Boardwalk in Atlantic City. There were no facilities set up for the mass number of troops, but there were hotels. "They put us all up there for the thirty days. Instead of a Quonset hut, we were put in hotels … not bad." Whether it was learning to march on beach sand or down the main streets of small towns—even highways—everywhere you could imagine, US soldiers were being trained for a war with no end in sight. All day and all night long, the training was becoming a part of them that would last a lifetime. They were all now property of the US government.

Purple was sent on to Nashville, Tennessee, where he received his indoctrination into military life: the GI haircut, inoculations, guard duty, and the infamous KP (kitchen patrol). He was also given a rigid medical exam and numerous types of aptitude and physical tests to determine whether he was best suited for training as a pilot, navigator, or bombardier. Once his classification had been determined, he entered preflight training and Officer Candidate School for approximately nine more weeks in Maxwell Field, Alabama. The aviation cadet program to train pilots, navigators, and bombardiers was also very demanding. After his application and appointment as an aviation cadet, Purple was sent to Rochester, New York, one of the three classification and preflight centers established; the other two were in San Antonio, Texas, and Santa Ana, California. Purple was still just a kid, his eyes wide open and eager to learn.

Into the Sky: Primary Flying School

When the United States entered World War II in December 1941, the US Army Air Forces continued with the type of pilot training program it had established in 1939—primary flying school operated by civilian companies under contract, and basic and advanced flying schools operated by the USAAF. There were three phases: primary, basic, and advanced flight training. Each cadet received sixty hours of primary flight training in nine weeks before moving on to basic flying school and then advanced flying school.

During basic flight training, a cadet received approximately seventy hours in the air during an additional nine-week period. In addition to operating an airplane of greater weight, horsepower, and speed, he learned how to fly at night, by instruments, in formation, and cross-country from one point to another. It was an amazing amount of study in such a short period of time. At this point in Purple's training, it was September 1943, and it was decided that he would go to multiengine advanced flying school.

Advanced flying school prepared a cadet for the kind of single or multiengine airplane he was to fly in combat. Those who went to single-engine school flew AT-6s, a fighter trainer, for the first seventy hours during a nine-week period, learning aerial gunnery and combat maneuvers, increasing their skills in navigation as well as in formation and instrument flying.

Cadets assigned to multiengine school received the same number of flying hours and even learned some combat aerobatics and gunnery. Using the AT-9, AT-10, or AT-11, they directed their efforts toward mastering the art of flying a multiengine plane in formation and increasing their ability to fly on instruments only.

The successful completion of pilot training was a difficult and dangerous task. From January 1941 to August 1945, 191,654 cadets were awarded pilot wings. However, there were also 132,993 who were either disqualified or killed during training, a loss rate of approximately 40 percent because of accidents, academic or physical problems, or other causes.[2]

Those who graduated from flying school were usually assigned to transition training in the type of plane they were assigned to fly in combat. The transition training—usually lasting about two months—became their last opportunity to prepare for combat before they deployed overseas.

---

2 http://www.nationalmuseum.af.mil/factsheets/factsheet.asp?id=1675 March 2015.

Chapter 3

I've Done Things with a B-17 You Couldn't Imagine

Walnut Ridge, Arkansas, was the location of Purple's basic flight school. He was now a pilot trainee; a few hours of dual training and then some for single-engines flying the BT-13 Vultee trainer, his reasons for being there.

In March 1944, at nineteen years old, Vincent "Bill" Purple graduated from advanced flight school, and was given his wings and commissioned as a second lieutenant. He was given a thirty-day leave. Purple hadn't been home for more than a year and a half. Immediately after his leave, he was given orders to report to Sebring, Florida, for multiengine bomber training.

Purple was extremely impressed at his first sight of the B-17, the aircraft known as the Flying Fortress—weighing in at sixty thousand pounds and with a wingspan of 104 feet. *And it could really fly!* [3]

In April 1944, as the war raged on in Europe, Purple graduated with a multiengine rating—ready for war.

He was assigned his combat crew in Plant Park, Florida, with nine others: copilot, radio engineer, turret gunner, bombardier, navigator, top gunner, tail gunner, and two waist gunners.

---

3 http://www.303rdbg.com/crew-duties.html March 2015.

They were transferred to Gulfport, Mississippi, for another ten weeks of transition flight training to fly combat missions of ten to twelve aircraft formation flying. Here, as everyone prepared for real war, they were shot at with wood bullets from a P-40. They would practice more and more flying in tight formations for bombing raids, elements of three aircraft that join four more elements to make a squadron of twelve. All this intense training was completed for three hundred thousand airmen, including pilots, navigators, and bombardiers.

Then it was off to Savannah, Georgia, to pick up a new Boeing B-17 Flying Fortress. Purple was only twenty years old in July 1944 and the youngest of his group. They left Savannah to fly north to Fort Dix, Grenier Field, in New Hampshire for the first stop before heading overseas. That flight would take them right over Purple's home in Athol; he made three low-level passes over his family homestead in the B-17. Everyone there knew who was piloting, and they were all waving up at him and waving American flags. What a sight that must have been from the ground to see that amazing bomber overhead, piloted by twenty-year-old Purple.

After leaving Gander, Newfoundland, in a bad snowstorm, Purple and his crew flew the new B-17 for a twelve-hour flight at twelve thousand feet across the cold and unforgiving North Atlantic Ocean. More statistics: that flight burned 2,900 gallons of fuel before landing safely in Valley, Wales. From Valley, Wales, they were off again to Kimbolton, England, their new home base. Purple was now part of the 379th bomb group in England. It was September 1944.

Normandy Had Already Been Invaded, and the Race for Nazi Germany's Total Defeat Had Begun

There was no keeping up with what was happening in the war. Only the day's briefing mattered, nothing further. Your problems belonged only to that day. The big picture wasn't available. "Didn't make any difference," Purple said. Like most soldiers, he was concerned with only one day at a time—literally.

He was assigned a B-17 position in the 525th squadron. There were twelve planes per squadron, and they took off from Kimbolton for various combat missions. "No matter what, you were going to be shot at," Purple said. Upon returning from a mission, they were always met by Red Cross volunteers, who waited for the crews with coffee, scotch, or whatever was available. The days were incredibly long.

"If you got back at five o'clock in the afternoon, you'd been at it since two in the morning," Purple said. "They were long days of flying, bombing raids, and catching lots of flak." Before this, in 1942, it was presumed that bomber crews over Europe would complete only eight to twelve missions before they were shot down or reported missing. After a few months, the US Army Air Force determined that pilots were required to fly twenty-five missions to "complete their tour of duty." However, the Eighth Army Air Force pilots had only a 25 percent chance of finishing their twenty-five missions without being shot down, killed, or captured as prisoners of war. By the time Purple began flying over Europe, the United States had increased the flight minimums to thirty missions—and eventually raised them to thirty-five missions. "It didn't really matter that much to me," Purple said. "I had a job to do, regardless."

By the war's end, the Eighth Air Force had lost 4,145 bombers in the 10,631 missions flown and more than thirty thousand troops—most of them "just blown out of the sky," said Purple.

"After flying only about ten missions," recalled Purple, "the commanding officers felt I was capable as a lead pilot, and I was promoted to lead the 526th squadron." From November to May 1945, Purple flew the lead plane as the squadrons followed him deep into enemy territory. Being lead plane meant you were shot at first, the first to catch flak, the first plane into enemy territory, and the first to drop your bombs. The lead bombardier would "bombs away" first, and the others would drop theirs as well—all hitting their targets as planned.

"A typical five a.m. briefing of the day's mission would begin with everyone huddled in a Nissan hut," Purple said. "On one wall was a large map of England to Germany." Dark lines showed the dangerous flight path to be taken. "Departing Kimbolton to the southeast over the English Channel to regroup, we continued over Belgium and on to our targets in Germany." They would all receive their latest weather briefing and reconnaissance reports, everyone's watches would be synchronized, and they would be provided with everything they needed to know—including how to return in poor weather or with damaged aircraft. From there, it was off to their aircraft.

"Once assembled in our aircraft, a flare was shot up signifying the mission was on and we needed to start the engines. We waited for another flare to taxi into assembly and another flare to taxi onto the runway and take off thirty seconds apart." They would all assemble over their base to get twelve planes in each squadron. It was typical to have 150 planes all doing this at once at five miles apart. On more than one occasion, to "level off the squadron at various assigned altitudes usually between two thousand and six thousand feet, at times we would have to climb as high as necessary to avoid the vapor trails from all the aircraft joining up in formation." It sounded chaotic and must have looked it from the ground. But they were precise and professional.

The formations were close. "I've tapped wingtips just for the fun of it," Purple said, smiling. Being lead plane meant the others would follow his aircraft—not a heading or an altitude but his aircraft, his wingtip in particular. "Just follow along and don't hit each other," added Purple. The lead had the precise assigned altitude. The others in his crew attended the same briefing, so they knew what to expect. When they were closer to their targets, they would get in even closer—literally under each other's wings. A steady hand and some nerves of steel were in order. Heading into Germany, Purple would carry ten five-hundred-pound bombs or a one-thousand-pound bomb. Sometimes the mission called for incendiaries, using thirty to fifty smaller bombs. It was a nasty war.

Flying at high altitudes above 25,000–27,000 feet in 1942–1945 was difficult to imagine. The air temperatures at those altitudes can get so cold—in the range of -50 degrees Fahrenheit—that your flesh can instantly freeze to any metal it touches, or fingers can just break off. Pilots, navigators, and bombardiers of a B-17 operating in Europe in 1944 wore their officer's uniforms just under their A-2 flight jackets. They were comfortable because of the many layers, and they also had electric suits to wear. These suits would consist of everything needed, from booties to a head warmer that would be plugged into the aircrafts power supply. The waist gunners would be cautioned as they fired their guns through open window gun-ports while the freezing cold air rushed onto them. As if being shot at wasn't enough! This exceptionally cold air also created the necessity of wearing bulky leather and shearling jackets, as well as the pants we see in all the photos and movies.

More than seventy years later, many missions still vividly stand out in Purple's memory. He also was on many missions where his planes caught fire. Although all missions were perilously dangerous to the crew and aircraft, being the lead plane had the added stress of being able to jeopardize an entire mission.

One of the worst was "engine four flaming up at twenty-five thousand feet over Hamburg, Germany," Purple reported. They had just completed a bomb drop and were turning to head home when the engine on the far right wing caught fire. With plenty of fuel in the tanks to worry about, the possibility of a major explosion was very real—not to mention the dangers of flak and enemy fighters looking to finish them off. A wounded bird being shot at is still a kill if it goes down. Purple pointed the nose of the gigantic aircraft downward while keeping the flaming engine high and above the rest of the burning aircraft, known in aviation as a side-slip. Needing to be mindful of the aircraft's structural limitations, he slid the plane downward, losing altitude while his crew watched the engine burn, hoping it would go out before spreading to the fuel tanks in the wings. Purple held a steady hand down from twenty-five thousand feet to twenty thousand feet, fifteen thousand feet, and eventually to ten thousand feet, until the fire finally smoldered out—fifteen thousand feet of descending on fire, saving himself, his crew, and the aircraft for another day of war. Although it's still an amazing story, Purple doesn't get excited or dramatic when recounting the event. This was one of four missions for which he was cited when receiving the Distinguished Flying Cross.

The bombers were attacked regularly by either the Luftwaffe, flak, or both. Flak typically consisted of surface-to-air rockets, also known as eighty-eights (88 mm shells) that would detonate at certain specified altitudes determined by the shooter. There was just no getting around it: they were going to be attacked. However, they usually had US fighter planes to escort them as far as possible. The P-47 and P-38 were the primary escorts for most of the war. But their range was limited by their fuel supply and would allow them only a partial distance escort. Of course, the enemies knew our approximate distances and ranges of operations—opening up the entire bomb squadron to be attacked with only their own guns for protection. "Each B-17 bomber had gunners located at all locations. The bombardier in the nose, an engineer/gunner at the top turret of the plane, radio operator/gunner covering the rear, the ball turret gunner that swivels on the bottom, waist gunners on both sides and rear of the aircraft, and a single tail gunner … Just about everyone had machine guns and another primary task," explained Purple.

When the P-51 Mustang came out, they had longer fuel supply ranges. The Mustangs could go farther and offer longer protection, and they were also faster than their previous escort fighters. The bombers all loved the Mustangs. It must have been a beautiful sight for the B-17 crews to see the P-51 Mustangs flying up to meet them on their way— the Mustangs flying tight formations around them for protection.

On one horrendous mission to Hopsten, Germany, Purple's squadron was facing surface-to-air antiaircraft weapon defenses. Once again, the experienced and dangerous Luftwaffe was after them. Flak was going off all around them; there was no dodging it on a bomb run. You keep your assigned heading and altitude and fly right into them with your squadron following. On this one particular mission, the lead plane was Purple flying his B-17 named *Four of a Kind*. As Purple looked to his right, he saw his right wingman get shot down. There was nothing he could do about it except just keep going. As is protocol, the other element plane from the right flew into position and filled in the vacant spot. With black smoke and flak everywhere, *Four of a Kind* was under fire again. Looking to his left, Purple saw that wingman also get shot down before that spot, too, was filled in. A flak burst then exploded only a couple of feet in front of his plane—a little high. "You just kept on course flying into a wall of black smoke, flak, and fighter jets coming after you … holding steady and towards your targets," he said. They completed their bomb run and Purple's B-17, *Four of a Kind*, returned safely to Kimbolton. It was another of the four flights for which the USAAF would award Purple the Distinguished Flying Cross. These Hopsten raids are well documented.

The other mission the USAAF combined with Purple's Distinguished Flying Cross occurred on March 9, 1945. Of the 330 missions, this was number 297. Purple was lead pilot of a squadron flying into the raid on Kassel in Germany, one of four missions to Kassel. While flying past the IP, the initial point on the flight plan where the aircraft begin their approach to the target, the *Four of a Kind* was at an altitude of approximately twenty-six thousand feet. Purple looked out his window and, to his horror, saw another squadron of B-17s directly below them at only three hundred to five hundred feet. If they dropped their bombs, they would surely hit the aircraft below them. "I actually made a 180-degree turn before hitting the target and ended up making two actual passes over the target," said Purple. He explained that turning a squadron of B-17s takes some time and some space. He estimated that while the enemy was shooting them at, they needed nearly a five-mile radius to make the 180-degree turnaround.

On another mission, things were a little quieter. Their attackers weren't hitting them. The navigator was leaning into the tight quarters of the Flying Fortress and jokingly told the crew, "Herman isn't shooting good today." Within seconds of saying that, the navigator had the end of his finger shot right off—proving that Herman wasn't a bad shot after all.

Purple made three trips to destroy a ball bearing plant in Germany on a day he still calls "Black Thursday." It was a day when hitting the target was difficult but not hitting it was not an option.

Chapter 5

There Was Freezing, Flying, Bombing, and More Bombing

The B-17 pilots and crews were dressed for all types of situations—not only with heated suits but armored suits as well. They had magnesium plates sewn into their suits—basically bulletproof armor—adding another seventy pounds to the four layers they were already wearing.

But the armored suit protected Purple and his crew when they were hit with flak. A shot came through the rudder pedal and clipped Purple's boots. He didn't get hurt because of his heavy flak suit. Like most of those in his generation that went to war, Purple just shrugged it off; being hit with enemy flak was just part of the job.

Their targets usually consisted of three particular kinds of sites: airplane factories and aircraft, ball bearing factories, and oil refineries—especially oil refineries. Without oil, the enemy had no planes, guns, or machinery.

On February 3, 1945, Purple was part of a major mission consisting of 1,003 bombing aircraft in a line almost three hundred miles long, unleashing a barrage of bombs thirty seconds apart over Berlin. The line equaled the distance from Boston's Logan Airport to Washington, DC, an amazing feat of organization. The fuel alone would require 2,900 gallons per aircraft, calculating into more than 2.9 million gallons of fuel for just for one mission. The skills of organization for aircraft, bombs, bullets, men, food, living quarters, medics, water, and much more had to be properly planned. Waste and abundance was not an option.

The Monday, February 5, 1945, London edition of *The Stars and Stripes* included this report:

> More than 1,000 Fortresses of the 8th Air Force fashioned a flying wedge against Berlin Saturday to help the wedge of steel being driven from the East by the Red Army, when they rained 2,500 tons of bombs in the heaviest attack ever made on the German capitol by the 8th. Among the targets were Tempelhof Airdrome ... pummeled by part of the great air fleet which stretched almost 300 miles across the continent. It took 45 minutes for the bombers to cascade their loads on the city.[4]

The largest raid to date consisting of B-17s and B-24s was led by Colonel Lewis Lyle and was the Eighth Air Force's most destructive bombing of Berlin. Our Purple from little Athol, Massachusetts, was aircraft 13, having 990 bombers behind him ... Just amazing! They would repeat this destructive mission to the enemy's hometown three more times.

Purple flew into Berlin on February 26 and again on March 18, 1945. Valentine's Day 1945 found him six miles over Dresden, Germany, followed six days later by dropping more bombs with his squadrons over Nuremberg. All his missions were flown out of Kimbolton.

---

4 "8th's Blow Sets Berlin Ablaze," *The Stars and Stripes*, London, February 5, 1945, vol. 5, no. 80, page 1.

Bill Purple was part of the 379th Bombardment Group (H), and their claims to fame were impressive. They flew more sorties than any other bomb group in the Eighth AF. They dropped a greater bomb tonnage than any other group. They had a lower abortive rate than any other group in action from 1943, pioneering the twelve-plane formation that became SOP during 1944. "*Ol Gappy*, a B-17G, flew 157 missions, probably more than any other in the 8th AF." Many books are available on the 379th.[5]

The Eighth Air Force had three divisions: the First, Second, and Third. From March 1943 to April 1945, the Mighty Eighth flew bombers regularly to end the war. The Second Division consisted of B-24s. The other two had B-17s. They all used the new twelve-plane formation.

By April 8, 1945, Bill Purple had amassed 1,500 flying hours, including more than 300 combat hours, fulfilling his obligation to the war effort by flying the then required thirty-five missions. His group flew 331 missions. "You'd fly three, four days a week sometimes," he said. "Whatever it took."

Purple was ordered back to the United States, and on May 8, 1945, he was on a boat home from Southampton, England, when the news flashed that Germany had surrendered and the war in Europe had ended. The toughest part came later: learning about the horrors of the concentration camps, which he would tell me about seven decades later.

---

5 http://en.m.wikipedia.org/wiki/B-17.

Chapter 6

Earning the Distinguished Flying Cross

"Headquarters, First Air Division–General Orders

Number 393, Dated 14 March 1945.

Vincent J Piepol, 0825970 Captain, Air Corps, United States Army. For extraordinary achievement while serving as Pilot of a B-17 airplane and the lead airplane of bombardment formations on bombing missions over Germany, 5 November 1944, 9 March 1945, 18 March 1945 and 24 March 1945. On all those operations, Captain Piepol exhibited outstanding flying ability and singular determination, aiding in large measure to the destruction of important enemy installations. On each of these missions, the airplane in which this officer was flying sustained severe battle damage. In the face of the hazards and difficulties involved, Captain Piepol continued on to the assigned targets where bombs were released with accuracy. On all the operations in which he participated, Captain Piepol served with distinction. The courage, coolness and skill displayed by Captain

Piepol reflect the highest credit upon himself and the Armed Forces of the United States. Entered military service from Massachusetts.

BY COMMAND OF MAJOR GENERAL TURNER

The dangerous missions outlined above were as follows:
Frankfurt, Germany, November 5, 1944
Kassel, Germany, March 9, 1945
Berlin, Germany, March 18, 1945
Hopstein, Germany, March 24, 1945

Chapter 7

Is Life Going to Be Normal Again?

Purple left the military in September 1946. He then joined the reserves and flew with the National Guard until 1951. As Purple would later explain, "We flew only about once every two weeks, which was too easy to get into trouble."

On June 2, 1951, Bill Purple married Helen Brand in Athol, Massachusetts. They lived very happily until her passing in 2011. They have two children, Cindy and Phil, as well as many grandchildren and great-grandchildren. After his return, the war became a memory; it was time to work, feed his family, and put all his war efforts behind him—which he did for thirty years. Tending his business and starting a curling club, Purple lived life the American way—until around 1979, when he learned about the 379th Bomb Group having an informal meeting.

The 379th Bomb Group was formed as an official association. Purple was one of their presidents. There were six thousand soldiers in the group during the operation in 1942–1945. In 1990, six hundred came to the reunion. However, by September 6, 2014, attendance had dwindled to only thirteen. They had decided to disband the 379th Bomb Group forever in their *Contrails* magazine. For the few left, it was beginning to be too difficult to travel. Purple and the surviving members still called each other on Christmas Eve for a toast and a chat. The following poem was written by Edward "Ted" Grossmith as a tribute to the 379th Bomb Group, making the last page of the last magazine of *Contrails*.

Going Home
With clear Bomb racks
We turn off track
Back through the flak
Black clouds of ack-ack
Through Flocke-Wulfe packs
We're going home

We're trailing smoke
The radios broke
Two engines gone
But the missions done
Into the western sun
We're going home

The war is won
The flying done
For our young crew
It'll all be new
A family too
We're going home

The war we fought
The peace we bought
Kept foes at bay
At the end of the day
We all could say
We're going home

One more to be flown
The target unknown
Last flight into the sun
Soaring one by one
Eagles forever
Going home.

On September 13, 2013, Athol's Bill Purple was awarded the French Legion of Honor (*L'ordre national de la Légion d'honneur*). This is the highest decoration offered by the French government and was started by France's first consul, Napoleon Bonaparte, in 1802. Despite being generally awarded only to French nationals, the Legion of Honor can be bestowed upon foreign nationals who have served France or upheld its values and principles as many US citizens did during the war.

When asked if he got back into flying after the war, Purple responded, "No. Flying can be dangerous, you know." Purple still attends air shows and special military events.

Thank you, Captain Purple, for your service to our country!

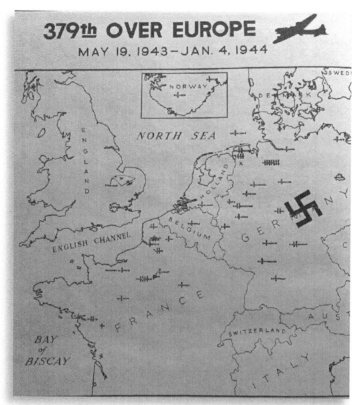

THE 379TH WOULD FLY OVER THE NORTH SEA TO REACH
GERMANY DURING THEIR BOMBING MISSIONS

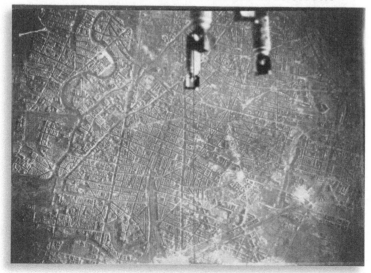

BOMB'S AWAY

DESTRUCTION OVER GERMANY

MISSED TARGETS

AMAZING DESTRUCTION

SURROUNDED BY DEVASTATION, A CHURCH
MIRACULOUSLY STILL STANDS.

CAPT. PIEPOL'S (PURPLE) OFFICIAL ID CARD

UNKNOWN DETAILS FROM CAPT. PURPLE'S

PERSONAL COLLECTION

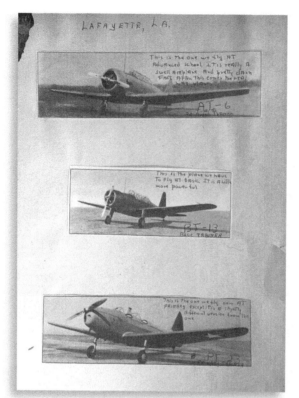

CAPT. PURPLE'S TRAINER AIRCRAFT

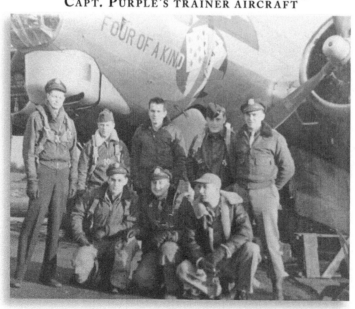

FOUR OF A KIND CREW, PURPLE BOTTOM CENTER

THE CREW OF *FOUR OF A KIND*

ON OUR WAY

SIMILAR B-17 FROM PURPLE'S COLLECTION

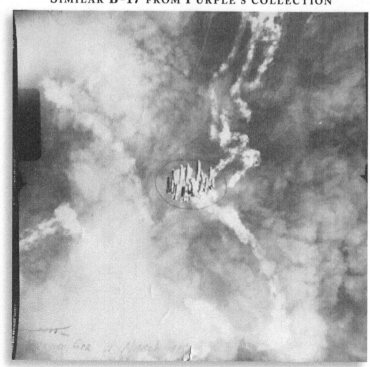

CLUSTER OF BOMBS AS THEY DROP MORE
HAVOC TO END THE WAR IN GERMANY.

CAPTAIN BILL PURPLE IN ONE OF HIS TRAINER AIRCRAFT.

Book 2

Corporal Fernand E. Frechette

Chapter 1

Who Is Fern Frechette?

Fern Frechette was born July 17, 1920, just after the war to end all wars—World War I—had ended.

Frechette's father, Clodiaux Frechette, was born in Worcester, Massachusetts. He had been living in Canada for a while with family when he met his soon-to-be wife, Rose. They were married and eventually settled down in Fitchburg, Massachusetts, where they raised four boys and three girls. Although his parents were born in Canada, they were all American citizens, proud and true.

Mom was a housewife, and Dad owned a barbershop in Fitchburg known as Frechette's Barber Shop on Daniels Street. One can only imagine what the barbershop conversations were like in the late 1930s as we watched from our safe shores as Hitler took over Europe and we fought off the Great Depression.

Of Clodiaux and Rose's four sons, only Fernand would go to war.

Frechette attended a Catholic grammar school, Saint Joseph's, in Fitchburg's predominantly French-Canadian section known as Cleghorn. However, he ended up completing only one year of high school. He was asked to drop out of school when his mom became ill and he was needed to help around the house with daily chores and taking care of the family. That was life in the 1920s and 1930s. Family and religion were soon to be his hope in life and humanity. He just didn't quite know it yet.

As we all know, the late 1930s and early 1940s brought the winds of another world war to US doorsteps. The unsettling year of 1942 was a whirlwind for America and Fern Frechette. He met and married Jeanette Godin, a beauty, on June 6, 1942. But war and the United States were calling, and Frechette was drafted only two months after his marriage. By October 2, 1942, he was serving the United States Army, not knowing if he'd see his bride again—soon or ever. He was just a kid at twenty-two years old.

Chapter 2

Reporting for Military Duty

Frechette reported at Fort Devens in Massachusetts and traveled with thousands of new soldiers for five days on a train to Camp Shelby, Mississippi. The trains would stop from time to time to feed the new soldiers. The Salvation Army provided quickly made sandwiches and hot coffee. A thankful Frechette remembered their efforts from that day onward, as the Salvation Army was always there to help. He traveled from Mississippi to Camp Polk, Louisiana, for basic training. From Louisiana he was sent to a camp in Arizona to train further for a secret US invasion planned in Africa. Finally, he embarked from New York City for the south coast of England to a town called Eastborne in February 1944.

By now, the troops knew their mission. While anticipating this great Allied attack, the wait and the fear of the unknown was very difficult. During this time, the Germans sent buzz bombs right over them to London. They saw the flash of fire coming from behind the bombs—bombs with their own engines. When they ran out of fuel, they'd just drop and explode. "Half of England was on fire," he recalled seven decades later.

US morale, as well as Frechette's, was always high. The soldiers would go into a pub and have beer, and everyone was very upbeat—even under such destruction and duress. They'd attend the USO and dances, with their orchestras playing. Keeping morale high was easy when you weren't fighting the enemy—at least not yet.

Corporal Fernand Frechette was now a member of General George S. Patton's Third Army. The signal corps was his primary assignment; their job was "to intercept copy and decipher the German codes." Morse codes were used, mostly. "Da-Di-da-Di-da" was the code he shared with me, even after all these years. He and his comrades worked out of a camouflaged green truck, with a big antenna sticking out of the top. They'd listen to ten receivers at a time through cheap military standard headsets. Once in a while, they'd turn the volume high to intercept a faint code, only to have some others come blaring through at the same time, as loud as thunder. As a result, Frechette has worn two hearing aids ever since.

Frechette was also part of General Patton's Third Army's "Ghost Army Twentieth Corps," a semifictitious troop that plotted to deceive the Germans into thinking the Allies were planning a major offensive attack at Calais, France. They had phony cardboard tanks and tents, rubber trucks, and airplanes. Speakers up on big telephone poles with amplifiers blared sounds of machinery and aircraft across the English Channel all the way to German-occupied France. They hoped the Germans would be listening. This pretend attack was staged to confuse the Axis Powers into thinking the big attack was imminent at Calais when it was actually planned for Normandy, France.

Normandy was still very well fortified with barbed wire, bombs, and beach protection, but less attention there would mean success for the world's most daring invasion. Frechette and his buddies were three thousand soldiers pretending to be thirty thousand, designed by television and theater set designers. Rubber decoy inflated tanks moved at night to make their unit look real, while they allowed enemy reconnaissance planes to just barely get a few photos of the incredible troops. Five of these studios were set up on the coastline to convince the Third Reich of the attacks. Hitler was correct; the Allies were planning a major attack. He just had the wrong location. Supreme Allied Commander General Dwight D. Eisenhower chose General George S. Patton to lead Operation Quicksilver, and it was brilliant—so brilliant, in fact, that it was sworn to secrecy for forty years. The United States knew the Cold War was coming, giving them potential reason to reuse this tactic.[6]

It was June 6, 1944. On D-day, Frechette was in England, where, he recalled, he saw the sky filling with aircraft. "There were thousands of planes, so many that they literally turned the sky black. When everything started up, we could feel the ground shake all the way to England." Then the orders came for his troops to head to Normandy, France.

By June 25, 1944, Frechette was in Normandy, D-day+19—nineteen days after the invasion of June 6 started. He remembers thousands of GI bodies just lying there, covering the beaches. The Germans had the area well fortified with bunkers on the hills, from which they shot down at soldiers on the beach as they left the amphibious landing crafts known as LSTs. "What a mess," Frechette recalled. They were only twelve miles inland at that point. Frechette again recalls the Salvation Army being there for the troops with coffee and even pens and paper to write back home. Then it was move forward whenever you could—no lying down or resting; just keep moving.

"General Patton was tough, very tough," recalled Frechette. At one point, orders came down from Patton that every soldier would connect their helmets using the chinstraps provided. "They'd better not get caught with them unstrapped." Unfortunately, the enemy troops knew this and used it to their advantage. Frechette explained how "the enemy would pull back on the helmets, breaking the necks of the soldiers." Patton soon realized that the straps proved more of a danger than a

---

6 http://www.generalpatton.org/d-day/patton_dday.htm.

safety feature, so he decided instead to allow his troops to ignore the chinstraps. However, Patton didn't relax on his requirement of having troops wear their neckties during combat. Frechette still shakes his head over that one—having to wear a necktie during battle!

Chapter 3

Surprise Attacks and Some Scary Times

Frechette was known as Frenchy to his unit. As he and his troops were advancing in France, they'd run into local French residents, and the soldiers would all gather around Frechette to hear him translate what was happening. They'd all give him questions to ask and then wait impatiently for his responses. "It was fun at first," he said, smiling at the memory of being in such demand.

Frechette turned twenty-three years old in Luxembourg while doing his job of copying and breaking codes. There were five companies to one battalion: Third Army, Infantry, Artillery, Tanks, and Signal Codes. There were about 120 soldiers in the company with Frechette, part of the Third Army's Signal Code Corps. When they received a coded transmission, they also needed to know the location of the code. That was accomplished using a direction finder by triangulating transmissions and locating the enemy—listening for their transmission and then locating their position. Depending on the information Frechette and his troops could attain, the US commanding officers would decide which action to take, "whether if bombing was needed or air strikes, or wait for more important valuable information to follow," Frechette said.

Everyone carried various firearms at all times. "We all carried arms ... That's what we were there for," explained Frechette, implying the obvious answer of war and killing.

Frechette vividly remembers being in full camouflage in the field, thinking they were nearly invisible. In what seemed to be an instant, they were spotted and attacked by strafing German Luftwaffe. Bullets were flying everywhere from the low-flying aircraft, meant to hit anything in their path. One of the soldiers yelled to "take cover." Thinking he was lucky to be near a truck, Frechette leaped under it for shelter. After the aircraft finished shooting and flew off, Frechette noticed he was crouching under the fuel tank of the truck. As if being strafed wasn't scary enough, he had taken cover under more explosives: gasoline. Smiling after all these years, he said, "I'll never do that again!"

In 1944, while in Luxembourg, Frechette had his first encounter with enemy troops. His company commander enjoyed a drink now and then—okay, more often than that, but could we blame him? Frechette was the only one in his company who spoke French fluently, so the first sergeant drove the jeep for the captain and had Frechette ride along. He recalled, "Visiting a farmhouse, there were two nuns and a small young girl on the side of a dirt road and the captain stopped to talk with them." Frechette's eyes were sore and hurting from the dusty roads. One of the nuns offered her sunglasses to him; it was an act of kindness that has always stayed with him.

Being the only French-speaking soldier, Frechette had been told a secret by the little girl: the barn behind them had German soldiers in it! There were only the three of them—the captain, the sergeant, and Corporal Frechette—and they were concerned about the situation. The captain had a couple of grenades and a sidearm pistol, the first sergeant had a carbine rifle, and Frechette had a submachine gun.

The barn was next to a hilly bank, and Frechette was ordered to climb it to overlook the doorway. The nervous captain threw one of his grenades at the barn, but it landed just short of the door. The captain and sergeant went to the door and nervously watched as the door swung open and a German soldier came out waving a white flag of surrender. Behind him was a line of armed German soldiers walking out with their hands up—more than thirty altogether, all marching out to surrender. This was the first time they had seen the enemy face-to-face; they were scared and, needless to say, very outnumbered. "If I'd had to pull the trigger, I don't think I would have been able to," Frechette recalled. "I was shaking so hard … I've never been so afraid in my life. The first German soldier I went up to, with my gun pointing at him … He had a machine gun too. I grabbed his gun, and he put his hands up. That's when about thirty more Germans followed him out. This was our first contact with German soldiers, and I was never so scared in my whole life."

With shaking hands and more courage than he ever thought he possessed, Frechette reached over and took the firearm from the enemy. Seventy years later, he still owns that exact weapon, given to his son Gary many years after the event. The Nazis were tired of fighting. Who knows how long they had been in that barn and what they might have had to eat, drink, and endure. The captain had Frechette get in the jeep to go get some troop support. Frechette smiled when talking how his legs were shaking and he could barely drive the jeep.

On a lighter note, the troops would joke about how awful the K rations were. The government-prepared food was all the soldiers had to eat. They loved their coffee, but fresh coffee was out of the question. They were given small packets of instant Nescafé coffee. "We'd use our canteen's cold water for mixing the instant coffee, and that's not coffee," he said, shaking his head. They also loved cigarettes and were given a package of three, a small candy bar full of nutrients, and a can of "whatever," Frechette added. "They gave us just enough calories. Taste wasn't as important as convenience."

Chapter 4

It Was Awful, Just Awful

Frechette and his comrades also had the difficult weather to deal with. "If it snowed, you'd lie down in the snow," he said, and it snowed a lot during those winters. "You went to sleep and your feet were cold. You woke up and your feet were still cold. If it rained, you were out in the rain, with no cover. Winter was awful. You were so cold, shivering, and wet. When we lay down, we'd just pass out shivering. You'd want to make a fire to warm up, but no fires were allowed at all. Jesus, it was tough," he recalled, looking off in the distance. "All the while, the enemy was out there waiting to find new ways to kill you and your troops."

All infantry traveled by foot or by 2½-ton trucks or jeeps. As a result of his ability to speak French, Frechette was fortunate to travel with the commanding officer by jeep many times.

Traveling by jeeps and motorcycles was also very dangerous because the Germans would string thin wire across the roads, affixing it to the trees. Many soldiers never saw it coming. The wire was just high enough to decapitate the troops in the front seats or the drivers of motorcycles and vehicles. Eventually, the United States used a modification, extending a three-foot vertical steel bar welded to the front bumper of the jeeps to break the decapitation wires strung across roads.

In Luxembourg, they continued their march during the winter of 1944. One of Frechette's fellow soldiers copied a code from the Germans about crossing the Nancy River. Frechette recalled seeing German soldiers in concrete bunkers along that river. The Americans were running out of supplies, so they were staying put for the time being. "We would see ambulances in and out of the bunkers, and at first, we didn't think much of it. Come to find out, they were bringing in artillery in those ambulances, getting ready to ambush us," he said.

Once his troops knew what was going on and they saw the Germans crossing the river, the soldiers knew they would have gotten caught in a bloodbath, according to Frechette. The deciphered code showed that a large group of Germans were planning to cross the river at daybreak the following morning. The message was sent up the chain of command. As a counterattack, the Americans loaded up their own troops during the night for an ambush the following morning. At his young age, it was very scary for Frechette to be part of the troops attacking these enemy soldiers. Some of his accompanying soldiers were only eighteen years old at the time, and it was certainly a terrifying experience for them.

"One kid intercepted a message that the Germans were coming, and if we hadn't gotten that message, we would not be here today," he recalled.

Frechette still smiles about the air corps and how they protected the ground troops. "They were great, just great," he said. The air corps would stay ahead of them for air protection. From the air, the pilots could see troops and their positions long before the ground troops could.

One time, they were advancing off the road and enemy trucks were scattered all around. The trucks were in flames, with bodies still in and on them. It must have been a horrifying and surreal sight. US aircraft came in low to strafe the area with bullets, ensuring none of them could attack Frechette and his friends.

At the beginning of the Battle of the Bulge, December 1944 to January 1945, Frechette's troops were heading to the Ardennes region of France. As they traveled, they spread out laterally rather than marching in one long line. Frechette was in a jeep, manning a .50-caliber machine gun. "A loud explosion went off in the distance, causing the truck in front of us to come to a panicked stop. It was nighttime, and other than the moon, the drivers would follow the dim lit taillights from the vehicle in front of them." Frechette's jeep collided violently with the 2½-ton truck in front of it. Frechette hit his head on his gun, and his helmet came down over his nose, breaking his nose and spitting his top lip. Blood splattered everywhere, and there was no medic was to be found. He lay down to rest his throbbing head and face. Fortunately, another vehicle was heading back to France with other injured soldiers and took Frechette with them. He remembered "looking up at the moonlit sky and seeing it get blurry until it disappeared," thinking he was going blind. He was bleeding so badly that "the blood was pooling up in my eyes and I wasn't able to see." Still, he offered no mention of pain or discomfort; he just stated the facts as they'd unfolded.

Finally transported into a medical tent, Frechette remembered a doctor talking with him. The doctor was telling him that he was from Haverhill, Massachusetts. Frechette liked that—a guy from home. The doctor also told Frechette he had a bone sticking out of the top of his nose before he clipped it off. The doctor then pushed what was remaining back into Frechette's nasal cavity. From there, the medicine man worked to sew up his lip. The man swore out loud, unable to find the right area to sew because of the blood running everywhere. Frechette spent ten days in the hospital in Paris before being shipped back to his outfit. He never heard of or saw the Haverhill doctor again. As far as the pain and discomfort, Frechette still didn't comment on any of it—nor did he mention whether he even received Novocain.

Once discharged and ordered back to his outfit, Frechette had to find them and was basically on his own to do so. He may have had a plan at the time, but seventy years later he didn't recall one. He did, however, remember the scary feeling of questioning everyone he saw, asking around to see whether anyone had seen American troops come by. But not all locals were friendly or willing to talk about the US troops' whereabouts. There were both Nazi sympathizers and Nazi resistance groups, and it was practically impossible to tell the difference.

Eventually back with his troops, Frechette advanced into France with his captain and sergeant, followed by the other 120 soldiers in his company. As the three of them advanced, they occasionally stopped, leaving Frechette by himself in the woods while the other two went back to retrieve the remaining troops. Frechette's orders were to "secure the area and hold it until the rest arrive." Although it was mostly Allied territory, he was as nervous as a squirrel with his eyes and gun darting back and forth in every direction. Oftentimes, he was visited by another US soldier looking to secure space for his troops as well. It's unimaginable to know what Frechette was feeling when he heard, "Wait here until we get back."

Chapter 5

Wagons of Bodies

B y April 1945, things had gone well for the Allies and the United States, but were terribly disturbing for General George Patton's Third Army and our Frechette. Originally ordered to Germany, the troops were heading for Berlin. They were on the autobahn when they received word they had to head south and reunite with other troops instead of heading directly into Berlin. Apparently, the Russian troops were entering Berlin, and it appeared that the US and British troops were being delayed from entering—possibly to allow the determined Russian troops to enter Berlin first. Everyone knew of the atrocities the Nazi army had afflicted on the Russians earlier in the war. Perhaps it was payback time? Frechette didn't know, nor was it his job to.

On the autobahn in the northern part of Germany, they headed south through Regensburg. As they went to Austria, the war in Europe was finally coming closer to an end.

Unfortunately, they were about to arrive at one of the worst murder scenes ever known to humankind: the Buchenwald concentration camp, near Weimar in Germany. "Every prisoner I saw in the concentration camps was nothing but skin and bones," Frechette said. "They had no food, no water, and lived worse than animals. The Germans were slaughtering them, throwing their bodies into a big hole and just bulldozing them—and some of them were still alive!" he said, with tears in his expressive eyes.

The US troops had just arrived. Buchenwald was one of the major concentration camps set up by the Nazis in 1937. Within twenty minutes of Frechette's arrival, the Nazis called many of the remaining POWs outside and riddled them with bullets before running off—trying to save their own skins and leaving no one to tell their story. The war was ending, and the enemy was scrambling to leave nothing behind.

At the concentration camp, Frechette helped liberate the remaining Polish prisoners of war—and right outside of France, they were all Polish prisoners.

Frechette was also at Buchenwald's subcamp called Ohrduf, where he witnessed incredibly charred bodies, starved beyond belief. There were more bodies that had been recently shot by the SS as they too ran for cover from the Allied forces. Frechette's photos are very disturbing, making it difficult to comprehend the treatment and murder of so many innocent people. The photos in this chapter were taken by him or men in his company as they saw the horror together for the first time. One photo is titled "Wagon of Bodies."

General Patton gave orders for all soldiers and civilians to walk past and see what had been done. "People that lived just outside the camps claimed they didn't know this was going on," Frechette said.

There were piles and piles of human bodies ready for bonfires. There were more on wagons just waiting for mass burials and more burning. Inside, he witnessed firsthand the massive lines of crematoriums, ovens designed for mass destruction of other humans—a terribly awful sight.

After the first visit to the concentration camp, the soldiers' fatigue turned to anger and was burned into Patton's Third Army.

The inmates had been either shipped to Auschwitz for annihilation or just worked and starved to death. Buchenwald remained one of Hitler and his Third Reich's major camps throughout the war. Although it wasn't an extermination camp like Auschwitz, they had inmates working in the armament factories nearby until they were either dead or had been killed by their captors—which was a regular occurrence. The exception was the Russian prisoners; they were just killed and cremated there.

Buchenwald was also made infamous by Ilse Koch, wife of camp commandant Karl Koch. She had a fancy for prisoners' tattoos and would often have them flayed from the victims and preserved, sometimes as lampshades. Jews and Gypsies were transported from Buchenwald to extermination camps farther east for annihilation. Later, as these camps were overrun by the Soviet Army, prisoners were crammed into Buchenwald. Some 13,000 of them died during three months in 1945 alone. The total death toll at Buchenwald may never be known, but it was well over 51,000. Between July 1938 and April 1945, some 240,000 people were incarcerated in the camp by the Nazi regime, including 168 Western Allied POWs.[7]

The camp was actually liberated by the US Army on April 11, 1945. Patton's troops found that the inmates had already taken over the camp after most of the SS guards fled. Buchenwald was one of the first glimpses that Americans had of the horrors of the concentration camp system. After the war, the Soviets used Buchenwald as a "special camp" for German and other political prisoners, some 7,100 of whom died there from 1945 to 1950.

"We, as American soldiers, would oftentimes offer a POW a cigarette," Frechette said solemnly, recalling the contrast between the two sets of troops. "The Germans would just shoot you. It was awful. The Germans would shoot you until they ran out of ammunition," he added, "and then call you their *kamarad* in German as they put up his hands in a mock surrender to their new comrades."

---

7 https://en.m.wikipedia.org/wiki/Buchenwald_concentration_camp.

After the Buchenwald liberation, Patton declared "no more prisoners." But there were prisoners still being taken, and signs broadly posted warned troops not to fraternize with any prisoners. Frechette said, "That was for the birds ... We offered them cigarettes and treated them properly."

One of the German POWs was wearing a watch and Frechette didn't have one, so he told the POW he wanted his watch. The German tried to communicate to Frechette in German, begging him not to take it. Frechette respected his wishes and left the POW alone, even knowing, he told me, that if the roles had been reversed, that watch would have been ripped right off his wrist without a second thought.

I Came Back Nervous All the Time

Corporal Fernand Frechette was in Austria on December 9, 1945. His time of duty was up, and he was sent to Chesterfield, France, for debarkation back to the United States. In total, he served almost three full years of wartime military duty. He returned to Miles Standish, Massachusetts, wearing his Ruptured Duck pin that would signify he was in uniform but discharged from the military. Upon coming into port, and having eaten K rations for three years, he was surprised when the soldiers all received a nice steak dinner.

Frechette took many photos that display firsthand the atrocities of World War II. They include images of the soldiers liberating concentration camps only to find bodies piled up in preparation for mass burnings, memories that will probably haunt this wonderfully humble man to his last day. Some photos are of him and some are of his friends; others are of his trucks covered in camouflage with them copying codes inside—many of the photos were stamped *Secret* on the back.

From Miles Standish, Frechette was sent to Fort Devens in Massachusetts. While turning in his uniforms and miscellaneous equipment, he found a book of unused bus passes. He took them, made his own pass to visit his wife, and made another one for his return to Fort Devens the following morning. The passes were supposed to be signed by a lieutenant. Frechette forged them using the name Walter Gordon, his father-in-law's name. He was finally reunited with his new bride.

Frechette worked for various companies after the war. He made rope at one company and clock cases in another. He finally retired from the city of Leominster after twenty-three years of service with the Department of Veterans Services, taking veterans to hospitals and doing anything else they or their dependents needed.

Frechette received many medals for his contribution: the Good Conduct Medal, the European, African, and Middle Eastern Campaign Ribbons, the American Theater Ribbon, the Victory Medal, and the Rhineland, Central European, Ardennes, and Black Forest Medals.

Even today, he still feels the fright of war, noting that when he returned home, he found himself jumping at noises that would not have bothered him before. "I came back very nervous all the time. After all these years, sometimes it still seems like it all happened yesterday." His wife would tell their children to not wake him suddenly, showing me how he'd awaken at any noise and jump, ready to fight. They have three children, Gary, Denise, and Alan.

Frechette brought home many items from Germany that he gave to his oldest son, Gary, who is also a military veteran. Frechette is a wonderful man who has made his wartime efforts his life, helping other veterans while knowing he's walked in their boots. Frechette still lives in Leominster, where we conducted all our interviews, and his home is military-style spotless.

Fernand Frechette is a class act. Recognized on July 5, 2014, at the Boston Red Sox "Hats Off to Heroes" program presented by John Hancock, our own Corporal Fernand E. Frechette was honored when the Red Sox took on the Baltimore Orioles.

Corporal Frechette, we can't thank you enough for your service to our country. Men like you have made a difference for generations. Thank you.

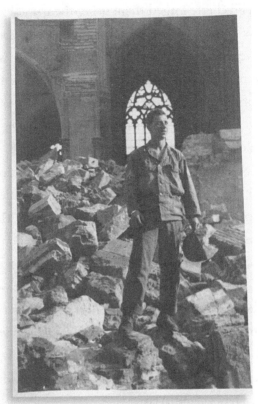

FRECHETTE AMIDST RUBBLE

ONE OF MANY FRECHETTE'S DUTIES

FRECHETTE ENJOYING KP

FRECHETTE ON RIGHT

FRECHETTE'S RADAR TRUCK

BREAKING CODES

BUCHENWALD CONCENTRATION CAMP HORRORS

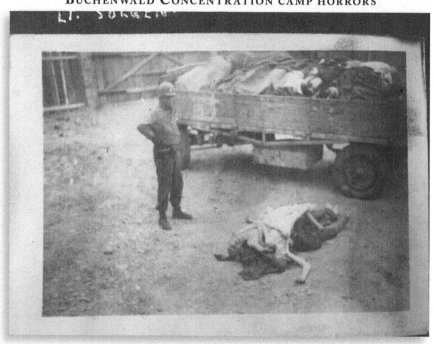

WAGON FULL OF STARVED BODIES

WITNESSING THE ATROCITIES OF WAR

"AWFUL, JUST AWFUL"

REMAINS OF HUMANS

MINUTES BEFORE FRECHETTE'S CREW ARRIVED AT BUCHENWALD

SOLDIERS LOOK IN HORROR AT PILES OF HUMAN BONES.

CREMATORY.

THE CREMATORY'S WERE VERY SMALL
AND LINED THE WHOLE WALL.

MACHINE GUNED BY S.S. TROOPS.

THE S.S. KNEW THE AMERICANS WERE CLOSE BY AND MASSACRED MOST REMAINING "WITNESSES" WITHIN MINUTES BEFORE LIBERATION.

HORRIFIED

THE DESTRUCTION OF FRANCE AND EUROPE WAS
OBVIOUS WHEREVER FRECHETTE HAD TRAVELLED.

FRECHETTE GRATEFUL TO TAKE A REST
LYING DOWN FROM THE WAR.

Book 3

FIRST LT. THOMAS J. AND ELAINE McDONALD

Chapter 1

Meet the McDonalds and Their Inspiring Stories

Thomas J. McDonald was born in Boston on February 12, 1923. He was one of six children of Peter and Marie McDonald. His father, Peter, was a WWI veteran who was given a Purple Heart for injuries suffered during that war.

Thomas McDonald's story here is different from the rest in that it includes accounts from his wife of more than fifty years, Elaine (Waugh) McDonald. Although Thomas passed away in 1994, he kept meticulous records and diaries during his war years, which Mrs. McDonald shared with me, along with her stories. Her perspective as the wife of a prisoner of war is certainly worth noting. The McDonalds efforts, sacrifice, and loyalty should never be forgotten or altered over time. It was real.

Mrs. McDonald recalls President Franklin Roosevelt's radio speech about the unprovoked bombing of Pearl Harbor by the Japanese and the words "a day that will live in infamy" bringing worry but also much pride to everyone. "We figured since they hit England, we'd be next, because they had missiles to hit us at home."

In 1940, Thomas McDonald graduated from a Jesuit high school, Boston College High. He went to university prelegal school for about three-fourths of a year. McDonald wanted to join the army and become an aviation cadet, but he was told he didn't have enough college education to qualify. He went to work in machine operation for Pratt and Whitney before enlisting. During this time, Elaine Waugh was working at New England Regional Life Insurance Company in Boston. Thomas and Elaine were already dating then, but as was the case of most Americans, their future started to become quite uncertain.

McDonald enlisted in the United States Army in June 1942. By September, they got to officially swear him in. The following is from his notes: "On 1 March, I was called to active duty in Boston Corps Area One. I received navigation training and was sent to Selman Field, Monroe, Louisiana. At the end of March, I took preflight classes and graduated. I was sent to Pyote, Texas, for a month, then to Dyersburg, Tennessee. I went overseas April 1 1944, I flew nine missions in combat and was shot down." I imagine it was not quite as simple as he portrayed it.

Thomas Joseph McDonald was called to active duty in Boston on February 27, 1943, to serve the "Duration of War and six months."

McDonald attended preflight school bombardier-navigator classes and received his Navigator's Diploma on June 4, 1943, from the Army Air Forces Classification Center in Nashville, Tennessee. The requirements, classification, training, and duties of air force personnel are broken down into specific details there.

The introduction to the Classification Center reads, "The primary functions of the Army Air Forces Classification Center are to classify Aviation Cadets for training as Bombardiers, Navigators, and Pilots, and to give the military and physical training to prepare them for specialized air crew schools.

"The training of the Navigator requires a minimum of 21 weeks, or approximately 5 months, including the original period at the Army Air Forces Classification Center."

The navigator's job is to determine the course the plane will follow and to direct it to its objective and back again.

Sigmund Sameth likened the job of the navigator to that of a bomber backseat driver. "Navigators used to be the forgotten men of the stratosphere. They were the guys who got the big ships there—and got them back. Their plotting boards meant success or failure for a mission as much as a bombardier's aim or a pilot's caginess in skirting 'flak.' Locating Japs pinpoint on the ocean through solid overcast miles from five miles up: setting a pilot back on course after minutes of tortured dogfighting: backseat driving a crippled bomber to Shangri-la with only the last gallon of fuel between you and the briny—those are vital air-war jobs today. But they don't make headlines."

McDonald was all set to go overseas before he was stricken with an emergency appendectomy on December 20, 1943. He wanted to marry Elaine Waugh before he left. She was thinking they would marry after the war was over; after all, she was nineteen and he was twenty years old. Nonetheless, during his sick leave, they were married on December 28, 1943, in Charlestown, Massachusetts. There was a wedding breakfast at the Lenox followed by a trip to the train station for a honeymoon in New York City. "They threw confetti and waved good-bye at us—like an old black-and-white movie," Elaine recalled with a smile. While on their honeymoon in New York, he contracted a staph infection that landed him in Governors Island Army Hospital. The honeymooners then enjoyed some three more months together. McDonald was eventually shipped overseas, headed for England on April 1, 1944.

In short, McDonald was a navigator for a B-17 bomber. He served overseas with the famed Eighth US Army Air Force in England for fourteen months as a combat navigator. Officially, he was a member of Eighth Army, 452 BG (bomb group), 728th Squadron. McDonald flew nine missions, totaling sixty-five combat hours. He was responsible for bringing the ship to the target area, as well as its safe return. He needed to be proficient in navigation by dead reckoning, celestial, pilotage, radio, and radar. McDonald was shot down over France on his ninth mission and taken as a prisoner of war, or POW. He spent eleven months as a POW before being liberated by the United States. McDonald accumulated approximately 550 hours of military flying time.

Ironically, he wrote the following in a V-mail to his wife dated April 17, 1944:

Well, I've been assigned an airplane. The name is *Why Worry*. I went to ground school again today and I imagine tomorrow will be the same. They are doing their best to keep us as busy as possible. We expect to have flown our first mission next week, so say a few prayers. If you should ever get bad news concerning me, don't lose faith because I'll get back to you somehow. We may get knocked down but the worst that will happen to me is I may be taken prisoner. Don't worry, I'll get back. It's been pretty cold here and those huts we live in are like ice boxes. The dampness goes right through you.

Chapter 2

Life and Love of a Navigator

McDonald was now a navigator in the *Why Worry?* and the crew was airborne, heading out on a combat mission. Following is a letter he wrote to his new wife as he directed the B-17 to ascend more than six miles into the air:

[Undated]

Monday

My Sweet,

I'm going up now. I'm up 8,000 ft., 9,000 ft. We're going up 2000 [feet] a minute. I just put my mask on I'm now at 13,000. Here after I wrote a number it will be thousands, 14,000 now and I feel a crackling in my left ear. We're going up 2,500 feet per minute now. Up 17,000 now. 18, 19, 20. I just turned my oxygen on full. There are twenty of us in here. Most of us have old type masks. The rest have new ones but it didn't fit tight enough. 24. The crackling in my ear has practically stopped and I feel perfectly normal. I think this is going to be very boring—26.5 27.5 I hope I can sit here for 3 hrs. 30.

They continued to thirty-eight thousand feet. All the while, Tom was writing to his wife about her clothes, about clicking his fingernails for signs of anoxia, which, he explained, could cause death. He wrote about her mother, Easter dinner, and how—if they lost their masks now—they would all be dead in forty-five seconds. He wrote again about his own mom and how he received information and regular letters from her. He went on about how his crew was getting the bends and starting to pass out. He still felt fine, by the way, but wanted to know who she was going dancing with. It was a tough flight for the crew; they were scared, knowing that "without oxygen at 28,000 feet for 6 minutes and you're dead usually." At that point, Tom clearly had two things on his mind: staying alive and getting home to Elaine.

Meanwhile, back home, Elaine would go to the movies to get updates from war clips. "We were just at war," she said. "You didn't look too far ahead. You just did what you had to do and believed in the president. Everything was scarce. There was no meat. We ate a lot of Spam. There was no sugar. We didn't have a car, so no gas rationing. We had the same friends we always had. Life went on … We went to dances and had our core group of friends."

Servicemen were everywhere during those days. She worked in Boston, and her boss was the head of the local Red Cross. He had converted the company's first floor into a blood bank. On her lunch hour, she'd go downstairs and register to help and to give blood. There was such a shortage of nurses that Mrs. McDonald ended up taking home-nursing classes. She would volunteer at hospitals and work for the Red Cross at night, packing items and supplies to be shipped to POWs. It was all done in the name of duty to her country; it was the new American way. But things were about to get worse.

On May 12, 1944, after McDonald's seventh mission, *Why Worry?* was shot down over the English Channel after completing an aerial mission. The B-17 heavy bomber was returning from Brux, Czechoslovakia. After completing the mission at twenty-two thousand feet, the B-17 was attacked and sustained extensive damage, forcing the aircraft to ditch in the English Channel. The crew members were in hostile danger on both the ground and in the air from enemy fire. The B-17 had been attacked in five waves of 150 to 200 German ME 109s and FW 190s, which caused great damage to the formations.

The ship McDonald was navigating had significant damage. It was hit in the number three and number four engines, the oxygen system was knocked out, the cylinders were ripped off, and the number four nacelle (outer skin of aircraft engine) had the skin ripped completely off. The rudders and stabilizers were nearly blown off. The ship was shuddering. There was a hit in the ammunition of the tail gunner, which exploded and cut the control cable back there. Only one aileron was working. The number four engine went out, the number three prop was feathered, and the number four was windmilling. Over the German coast, they lost the number one engine. Number two was still chugging along on emergency boost. Between Calais and Dunkirk, near Grandienes, the ship was losing altitude and they were forced to ditch, eight miles off the French coast in the minefield.

"It was through the efforts of Lt. McDonald and the application of the principles of navigation by him, that guided them over enemy country and into friendly waters. It was also through his skill that the radio operator was able to send out the coordinates of their location when forced down, which brought about their speedy rescue, with no injury to members of the crew," reads a citation from his commanding officer. McDonald had to *parachute into the waters,* explains another citation.

More newspaper reports followed: "WHY WORRY? B-17 of the 728th Squadron, May 12, 1944. Attacked by a horde of enemy aircraft the Eighth Air Force Flying Fortress, Why Worry?, piloted by 2nd Lt. Milton Mard of Jersey City, New Jersey, crash landed in the English Channel with two of its gunners seriously wounded and three of its four engines out."

Another firsthand account written by right waist gunner Joseph L. Soucy is included in a book titled *We Were Eagles, Vol. 3, The Eighth Air Force at War, June to December 1944*, by Martin Bowman, "*Why Worry?* in the 728th Squadron, piloted by 2nd Lieutenant Milton M. Mard of Jersey City, was attacked by a horde of Fw 190s and Bf 109s."

Soucy is quoted in the book as follows:

> A lot of things happened fast. A very sickening sight I saw was a guy who had bailed out, but pulled his ripcord too soon and his chute got tangled in the prop of a plane below his and ripped his chute right off his back. All there was left was a few pieces of cord waving in the breeze and there he was looking back at it on his way down. We were getting hit by then, they were shooting at us and us at them.
>
> On the first pass, enemy machine-gun fire put out two of *Why Worry?*'s engines out of operation. On the second pass, the rudder and horizontal and vertical stabilizers were nearly severed and the oxygen system was knocked out. A 20-mm shell exploded in the left waist and wounded the gunner. His left hand, shoulder and right eye were bleeding profusely. Another shell struck Joseph Soucy. He was hit in the neck, upper right arm and left leg. Although in great pain, he said nothing about his wounds so that he would cause no anxiety for the rest of the crew. Instead, he remained at

his gun, firing with his one good hand, and blew up one enemy fighter and probably destroyed another. Tearing through the tail section, another shell exploded in the ammunition box and set off a belt of rounds. "It scared the hell out of me," joked the tail gunner, Sergeant Martin A. Smith. "I almost thought it was good old American 4th of July."

Joseph L. Soucy continues:

A 20-mm shell hit the left waist gunner's machine gun, exploded and a chunk of steel went up his arm between the two bones of his forearm. He then went to the radio room and was using that gun with his good hand. I was still at my gun trying to keep off the bandits. It was then I found out that we had only two engines running and one of them wasn't running too well. The word was passed to use up all our ammo and to drop the ball turret. It seemed that everyone was too nervous to do anything so with just my good left hand, I dropped the ball turret. I was later told that by dropping the ball turret, the plane gained 15 mph speed, just enough to get us to the English Channel. There we ditched our plane, hitting the water with a crash. Since my right arm was no use, I didn't think I could pull myself out of the top escape hatch to the radio room. The plane being torn open, I just walked right out through the side, hanging on. Then I pulled the cord on my Mae West but unknown to me, the thing was full of holes and just fizzled. Someone yelled that the plane was rolling over on me and to get away from it. I let go and went down. Being fully dressed and with only one good arm, I could not manage to stay up so Martin Smith jumped into the water to help me stay afloat until a dingy could be found to keep me up.

While the radio operator, Private Royce E. Heath, was administering first aid, the third engine went out. "When that went out," stated the bombardier, 2nd Lieutenant William D. Blades, "my heart seemed to stop. We had only one engine to crawl back home on." Because of the inoperative oxygen system, the crew took turns sniffing from two emergency bottles for the remainder of the hectic trip. During this time the ship wanted to constantly nose up, causing additional trouble. *Why Worry?* dropped its bombs on the target and left the formation for her home base. A P-47 drew up close and escorted the limping Fort. "The P-47 was a wonderful creature," commented the navigator, 2nd Lieutenant Thomas J. McDonald. "It made us feel like we were in mother's arms."

In sight of the English coast, the ship could no longer limp and Mard announced they were going to ditch in the Channel. "We skipped along like a toboggan on a toboggan run," recalled the top turret gunner, S/ Sergeant George Boyce. *Why Worry?* nosed down and then hit the water. "We paddled one of our dinghies around and picked them both [Soucy and Smith] up," said Sergeant Edward Koster. "It was a great thing for Sergeant Smith to do," commented Koster, "for he is a little fellow, weighing only about 150 pounds." The crew was picked up by Air Sea Rescue and rushed to a hospital on reaching the English coast. Ditching in the Channel qualified the entire crew as members of the "Gold Fish Club," an exclusive club reserved for crewmen who have to ditch in the water or bail out in the "drink."[8]

---

8 *We Were Eagles, Vol. 3, The Eighth Air Force at War, June to December 1944,* by Martin Bowman and published by Amberley Publishing, February 15, 2015.

Twelve Days Later, Shot Down a Second Time

On May 27, 1944, *Why Worry?* went down again, this time in enemy-occupied France. His ninth and final mission left McDonald with another concussion from hitting his head and becoming unconscious. He was reported to his wife and the public as MIA, or missing in action. His whereabouts were still unknown to the US government. He may have been alive and wandering the woods in German territory, captured as a POW, or dead like many others.

On June 7, 1944, Mrs. McDonald received the following telegram:

Reported Missing in Action

The Secretary of War desires me to express his deep regret that your husband Second Lieutenant Thomas J Mc Donald has been reported missing in action since twenty seven May over Germany if further details or other information are received you will be promptly notified

The Adjutant General

The local newspaper also ran an announcement about the missing soldier, saying McDonald was navigator of a B-17 bomber that was missing over Germany. The announcement read like an obituary, including when he was married, and when he'd graduated from Boston College High School and Suffolk University.

Once McDonald regained consciousness, he was able to walk away from the ship, this time only to be captured by German soldiers four hours after the crash. He was now a prisoner of war in Germany.

Sometime thereafter, Mrs. McDonald received her second telegram. This one significantly changed things at home for her.

> Report just received through the International Red Cross states that your husband, Second Lieutenant Thomas J McDonald, is a prisoner of war of the German government
>
> Letter of information follows from Provost Marshal General

The wives and next of kin of POWs joined together, a close-knit group that would pack and ship items when allowed to their loved ones. American Prisoner of War Next of Kin Meetings were a regular occurrence now for Mrs. McDonald.

McDonald's B-17 went down on May 27, 1944. On August 10, 1944, Mrs. McDonald received another telegram about her husband's internment:

> RE: 2nd Lieutenant. Thomas J. McDonald United States Prisoner of War, Stalag Luft 3, Germany

Dear Mrs. McDonald:

The Provost Marshal General has directed me to inform you of the transfer of the above-named prisoner of war to the camp indicated.

You may communicate with him by following instructions in the enclosed mailing circular.

One parcel label and two tobacco labels will be forwarded to you every sixty days without application on your part. Labels for the current period will be forwarded under separate cover.

Further information will be forwarded as soon as it is received.

Sincerely yours,

Howard F. Breses,
Colonel, C.M.P.,
Assistant Director,
Prisoner of War Division

Chapter 4

POW Stalag Luft III, Germany

Second Lieutenant Thomas J. McDonald's new home was German POW camp Stalag III, in barracks 168, room 12—which was no more than a hut ten feet by twelve feet. Inside, five triple-decker bunks were home for fifteen airmen. By liberation, eleven months later, more than eleven thousand airmen would call Stalag III their home. The camp would eventually consist of five separate compounds: North, South, East, West, and Center. McDonald was in the South compound with American airmen.

The Germans were determined to make the camp inescapable. They built all the floors more than two feet above the ground, allowing guards to look under each hut for anything suspicious. The soil was soft and sandy, making tunnel digging almost impossible—as the sand could cave in easily. Lastly, the topsoil was gray in color and the soil beneath had a distinctive yellow tint—another difficulty the POWs would have to deal with to conceal any earth displacement from tunneling. The camps were intentionally located on sixty secluded acres.

There were several famous movies pertaining to Stalag escape attempts and POW life. *Stalag 17* starring William Holden was made in 1953, and *The Bridge on the River Kwai*, also with Holden, came out in 1957. *The Great Escape*, released in 1963, was based on one of the actual escapes from Stalag III. These films could be considered the top three POW movies of all time by critics and audiences alike.

Stalag III was one of the best-organized POW camps in German-occupied territory. It had a recreational program that included soccer, basketball, and other sports. It also had an extensive library; McDonald used his time there to learn Spanish.

There were eight hundred Luftwaffe guards; they were either too old for battle or young convalescing soldiers. The POWs called them goons. The Germans didn't have a clear understanding of the English language and were told that *goon* stood for "German officer or noncom." The POWs followed the goons around at all times, taking notes of their movements and locations to aid in their plans to escape.

Tom McDonald wrote often to his new wife from his new home: Stalag III. Calling it his "permanent address," he explained the rules of communications and how he could send three of the letters supplied to him and four postcards each month. In exchange, he was allowed to receive a package not to exceed eleven pounds. In it, he asked for "oatmeal and stuff like that."

Elaine was able to correspond with him directly, and his letters would reach her. However, "they'd black out what they didn't want me to read," she recalled later, "to frustrate us back home or something in case we were spies." It only frustrated her more, as half the letter would be blacked out from the censors. She shipped him cigarettes and other tradeable items, as Tom often traded his cigarettes for chocolate bars; he attributed those small bartering sessions with the German soldiers with saving his life while a POW. The Germans loved to trade, and all was fair game. They'd hardly feed the prisoners, and relied on the Red Cross and family packages to increase their daily caloric intake. Fortunately, the POWs of Stalag III pooled and split their packages and supplies for the common good.

In another letter dated June 20, 1944, from Stalag III, McDonald explained how boring life was as a POW: "I have finally gotten into the swing of things here. I take Spanish and do quite a bit of reading besides playing ball or something each day. The hardest task around here is finding something to keep you busy. It is very easy to get lazy and out of shape."

On June 28, 1944, McDonald wrote again: "I have now been down one month ... tomorrow we'll have been married six months. I wish the second three months had been as happy as the first, but we will see those happy days again and the memory is wonderful. The Fourth of July is drawing near and there is quite a program planned. We'll have everything but the scotch and the dancing girls ... keep your chin up and pray for peace. I'll see you soon. With all my love forever, Tom."

Meanwhile, back in Charlestown, Massachusetts, Mrs. McDonald continued packing supplies and the items needed and allowed for her husband and other POWs. She continued to attend the American Prisoner of War Next of Kin meetings at the First Corps Cadet Armory at 105 Arlington Street in Boston, a support group sponsored by the Red Cross for the next of kin and civilian internees.

By August 3, 1944, the US War Department was concerned about the treatment of POWs in German prison camps. While debriefing escaped soldiers, they were told the daily diet consisted of the following: breakfast—nothing, served with water if wanted; lunch—a bowl of soup and one slice of bread, usually black with mold; supper—two potatoes. The American Red Cross sent food to the prisoners every week or so, and without their contribution, prisoners would have starved. Reports showed that most were suffering from malnutrition.

The Germans oftentimes waited up to five days before feeding their new POWs. They even told the British that the Americans were not willing to share their Red Cross packages with them and told the Americans the same about the British, all to cause havoc and distrust among the Allies.

Chapter 5

Gefangenen Gazette, POW Magazine

The prisoners of war actually had a newspaper of sorts called the *Gefangenen Gazette*. *Gefangenen* means "Prisoners" and the paper was "Published by the American Red Cross for the relatives of American Prisoners of War and Civilian Internees," according to the top of the special supplement to the prisoners-of-war bulletin.

Tom McDonald kept many original documents and files from his wartime efforts, including copies of the *Gazette*. One dated September 1944 estimated there were 4,500 American airmen at Stalag Luft III, where McDonald was being held. All the paper's material needed to be reviewed and accepted by the Stalag commander. However, Stalag III was a camp for airmen. This allowed them plenty of free time to read and study, compared with enlisted men, who had harder work details. Officers of this camp were under direct control of the Luftwaffe, German airmen.

Within the *Gazette* were stories of how medical treatment was difficult because of full hospitals; there were 490 patients, and another trainload of POWs was expected soon. A section called Gossip and Rumors was also included. Supposedly a POW had received a letter from his wife that said, "Darling, I'm having a baby but it's not yours. He is an airman too and he's very nice about it. He promises to send you cigarettes while you're there." Ideally, that was just a coded message, because the Allies were great at sending information back and forth. The wives and girlfriends of POWs were left with a difficult and unknown fate as well. The few reports coming back were never promising.

The paper also included details of German authorities searching the POWs' personal belongings at random; they weren't specific about what they were looking for, but it was obvious they had something particular in mind.

Another article with the headline "Dwindling stock of towels" explained that 109 towels were confiscated by the Germans and would not be replaced. It advised the prisoners not to turn in their "burnt, grimy, dirty, damp or torn towels" and to wash the towels themselves. Otherwise, they wouldn't get a replacement towel. Lightbulbs broken or burned out also would not be replaced, the article said.

The commandant also used the newsletter to make it clear that nothing should be thrown over the warning wire, a wire between the camp and the barbed wire. Cigarettes, trash, clothing or anything else were not allowed between the fences. The guards were to order the POWs to *Halt oder Ich schiesse*," which translates as "Halt or I shoot."

Further information was given that much of the mail had not been properly delivered, in or out of the camp. The Germans continued to censor everything. Then, of course, the rations were cut once again. Potato rations were cut by a hundred grams, macaroni and sauerkraut would no longer be given out, and they were replaced with kohlrabi. There was a cartoon and an article asking soldiers to please refrain from "idle chat," because the carelessness could claim Allied lives. Such was life as a German POW.

Promotion and recognition: On December 1, 1944, while still interned in Stalag III, McDonald was promoted by the United States from second lieutenant to first lieutenant.

Mrs. McDonald was notified on December 14, 1944, that by the direction of the president, she was to receive her husband's Air Medal and One Oak Leaf Cluster award on his behalf. In part, it read, "For meritorious achievement while participating in heavy bombardment missions over enemy occupied Continental Europe. The courage, coolness and skill displayed by this officer upon these occasions reflect great credit upon himself and the Armed Forces of the United States ... Since this award cannot be presented to your husband at this time, the decoration will be presented to you."

In keeping families back home respectfully involved, a ceremony was held at Headquarters, AAF Base Unit, Logan Airport Boston on January 18, 1945. A personal and proud letter from Captain Kasson W. Lawrence was presented. It read as follows:

> In presenting this award to you, our Government is expressing devout thanks to him and to you, his wife, for his outstanding courage and performance in the defense of our beloved country. His devotion to duty has been outstanding, and his qualities as a man and as a soldier make him worthy of our high praise. Any honor which you, Mrs. McDonald, that I, on behalf of the War Department and by Direction of the President of the United States, present this symbol of his bravery and of a nation's gratitude. When this war is finally over, and the deeds of brave men are recounted, your husband will be numbered among those who accepted the most dangerous tasks with unusual bravery and intelligence. And to them we will owe a great share of the credit in the task of ridding the world of barbarism and slavery. As you are justly proud to be his wife, so are we equally proud to claim him as a true son of liberty.

Back in Stalag III, as the war raged on, POWs could smell victory coming. They also had knowledge of the methods the Nazis were using in covering all their tracks and atrocities—causing the POWs to worry that they would be mass murdered to prevent eyewitness accounts.

McDonald was a POW from May 27, 1944, to April 29, 1945—for eleven months. Realistically, for McDonald it was 337 days—long days of trying to keep busy for the sake of his health, mind, and spirit.

Sometime just before midnight on January 27, 1945, the Germans marched eleven thousand prisoners to Stalag VII-A, in Moosburg. The POWs went thirty-four miles and arrived in Bad Muskau, where they rested for thirty hours. They continued to walk the remaining sixteen miles the following day.

From one account on Wikipedia, "The Russian army pushing in from the east caused the Germans to evacuate the camps and made the prisoners walk to the southwest, as snowflakes portended a blizzard. Snow fell for four days in near zero temperatures. With frozen feet and hands and sickness, many died along the way. Six days and sixty-two miles from Sagan, they reached Nuremberg. To add to their misery, there were air raids at night—lice, bedbugs, fleas, food shortages. Diarrhea and dysentery also ran rampant."

Fortunately, McDonald was in the South compound, which meant he didn't end up on that march. Instead, he was put on a boxcar and taken to Stalag II-A. The Germans crammed about fifty men on a boxcar that was seven by twenty-five feet long. They were allowed only water once during their journey. The regular "delousing" of the new POWs at Stalag II-A occurred on April 9.

Chapter 6

Final Nazi Push and Liberation

The war was getting close to ending, and the Germans were on the move east. As indicated, they had taken some of the POWs and had them march in close formation while German soldiers walked loosely around the GIs. At times, the American aircraft assumed the "marching troops" were Germans and strafed them, killing many of their own soldiers. The German plan often worked as intended.

Sensing defeat, the Germans proposed an armistice, but it was rejected. It involved allowing the Germans to retain their weapons. More fighting ensued, but by that time, the German forces were weak, with small arms and minimum ammunition—and were easily overpowered by tanks, cannons, and the US Sixth Army. Many German soldiers were quick to surrender, including the 240 prison guards left at the largest and once-proud German prison camp, Stalag VII-A.

The stay at Stalag VII-A lasted about four months until Combat Command A of the Fourteenth Armored Division took the surrender of the camp garrison. Initially, they reported the number of prisoners liberated as 27,000. This was wrong; there were more than 130,000 Allied prisoners liberated from Stalag VII-A, the war's largest prisoner-of-war camp.

The war in Europe finally ended with the full and total surrender of Nazi Germany to the Allied armies on May 8, 1945. It was almost time to go home.

May 25, 1944: The commanding officer of the 728th Bomb Squadron had put Tom McDonald's name in for the Oak Leaf Cluster to Air Medal award based on the water ditching that occurred on May 12, 1944, as described previously. The report from the commanding officer read, "Combat over enemy occupied territory, fighter attacks, concentrated enemy aircraft, and anti-aircraft fire, drowning or further damage or injury in ditching in channel. The courage, skill and tenacity of purpose of Lt. McDonald reflect the highest credit upon himself and the Armed Forces of the United States."

First Lieutenant Thomas McDonald went overseas on April 1, 1944. During that time, he flew nine missions. McDonald's B-17, *Why Worry?* made forced-off-field crash landings on two occasions—May 12, 1944, and May 27, 1944—resulting in injuries on both occasions.

McDonald was only on his seventh mission when his crew was forced to ditch the plane in the English Channel. On May 27, 1944, they crash-landed in France, where McDonald was knocked unconscious. He was able to walk away from the ship but was taken as a German POW only four hours later.

After being liberated, all POWs were given a sixty-day recuperation leave—sixty days to learn how to deal with the scars, the difficulty, and the nightmares of being held captive by ruthless enemies. The war was still going strong in the Japanese theater, and all the troops in Europe knew they would be headed to the South Pacific. That war was getting bloodier and more drawn out. The atomic bomb wasn't dropped until August 6 and again on August 9. Japan surrendered fully on August 15, 1945, ending World War II. It was the only time in history that nuclear bombs were used during warfare.

According to medical records dated October 9, 1945, McDonald was eligible for the award of the Purple Heart. On November 29, 1945, during a formal hearing, he asked to be honorably discharged and retired from service because of headaches and fatigue from battle injuries and internment. Three doctors agreed with him, but one did not, so the request was denied. On December 6, 1945, he was granted a temporary limited service for six months but found comfort at being excluded from any further overseas service.

McDonald was honorably discharged from the United States Air Force on April 24, 1946. He logged 500 hours as a B-17 navigator during war. His service lasted two years and six months—921 days of military service, of which 337 days were spent as a German POW. Days were more representative than years or months; all service members lived only one day at a time, concerned only with the day's mission. For many, tomorrow never came.

During the war, the United States averaged a loss of fifteen thousand men per month—brothers, fathers, uncles, and friends who never returned.

After Tom was discharged, the McDonalds were reunited and traveled back east together by train. They were fortunate again. Reservations were unavailable and seating was tight, so everyone wanted to get on the trains. Elaine recalled, "That was a happy time. We'd call for a porter, and for fifty cents, they'd do anything. They always had a bar at the end of the train for drinks, and the dining was so good."

Upon returning to Massachusetts, Mrs. McDonald found employment at Waterville Inn for the summer while her husband found work as a night watchman. Then it was back to school for McDonald on the new GI bill. In 1948, McDonald graduated from Suffolk University, and in 1957, he earned his master's degree from Boston College School of Social Work.

When he first returned home from the war, the McDonalds were told they'd probably never be able to have children. Happily, they beat the odds once again and had three boys and three girls. The elder two were given their parents' names—Elaine, then Thomas—and were followed by Elizabeth, Peter, Celine, and William. The couple decided to settle down in Bedford, Massachusetts. They borrowed two hundred dollars and, in 1950, purchased their first home.

For more than eleven years, McDonald was a director of the North Central Mass Mental Health Center in Fitchburg. He was a therapist at the Leominster Hospital School of Nursing and director at Middlesex County House of Correction, as well as the Supervising therapist at Massachusetts Correctional Institution.

McDonald lived a life full of family and helping others. Thank you, Lieutenant McDonald, for your sacrifice and service to all Americans.

CREW OF THE *WHY WORRY?*

NOSE ART OF THE *WHY WORRY?*

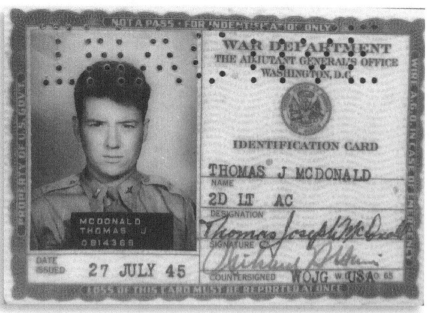

OFFICIAL MILITARY ID CARD OF THOMAS MCDONALD.

WB178 34 GOVT WUX

WASHINGTON DC 107P 29

MRS ELAINE M MC DONALD

25 MEAD ST CHARLESTOWN MASS

REPORT JUST RECEIVED THROUGH THE INTERNATIONAL RED CROSS STATES

THAT YOUR HUSBAND SECOND LIEUTENANT THOMAS J MC DONALD IS A

PRISONER OF WAR OF THE GERMAN GOVERNMENT LETTER OF INFORMATION

FOLLOWS FROM PROVOST MARSHALL GENERAL

ULIO THE ADJUTANT GENERAL

YOUR HUSBAND IS A POW.

WB141 44 GOVT

WASHINGTON DC 1144A 7

MRS ELAINE M MC DONALD

25 MEAD ST CHARLESTOWN MASS

THE SECRETARY OF WAR DESIRES ME TO EXPRESS HIS DEEP REGRET THAT YOUR

HUSBAND SECOND LIEUTENANT THOMAS J MC DONALD HAS BEEN REPORTED MISSING

IN ACTION SINCE TWENTY SEVEN MAY OVER GERMANY IF FURTHER DETAILS OR

OTHER INFORMATION ARE RECEIVED YOU WILL BE PROMPTLY NOTIFIED

ULIO THE ADJUTANT GENERAL

YOUR HUSBAND IS MIA.

MRS ELAINE M MCDONALD=

25 MEAD ST CHARLESTOWN MASS=

THE SECRETARY OF WAR DESIRES ME TO INFORM YOU THAT YOUR

HUSBAND 2LT MCDONALD THOMAS J RETURNED TO MILITARY CONTROL

29 APR 45=

J A ULIO THE ADJUTANT GENERAL.

2LT 29 45.

Tom – LIBERATED – APRIL 29, 1945

YOUR HUSBAND HAS RETURNED TO DUTY.

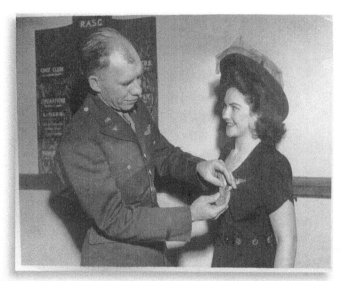

MRS. ELAINE MCDONALD ACCEPTING AN AWARD FOR THOMAS MCDONALD WHILE HE WAS A GERMAN POW

HEADQUARTERS
4102D AAF BASE UNIT
LOGAN AIRPORT
EAST BOSTON 28, MASS.

18 January 1945

Mrs. Elaine M. McDonald:

In presenting this award to you, our Government is expressing
devout thanks to him and to you, his wife, for his outstanding
courage and performance in the defense of our beloved country. His
devotion to duty has been outstanding, and his qualities as a man
and as a soldier make him worthy of our high praise. Any honor which
we can bestow upon him belongs also to you, his wife. So it is to
you, Mrs. McDonald, that I, on behalf of the War Department and by
Direction of the President of the United States, present this symbol
of his bravery and of a nation's gratitude.

When this war is finally over, and the deeds of brave men are
recounted, your husband will be numbered among those who accepted the
most dangerous tasks with unusual bravery and intelligence. And to
them we will owe a great share of the credit in the task of ridding
the world of barbarism and slavery.

As you are justly proud to be his wife, so are we equally proud
to claim him as a true son of liberty.

WASSON W. LAWRENCE
Captain, Air Corps
Commanding

CITATION TO MRS. MCDONALD ON BEHALF OF HER HUSBANDS "UNUSUAL BRAVERY AND INTELLIGENCE."

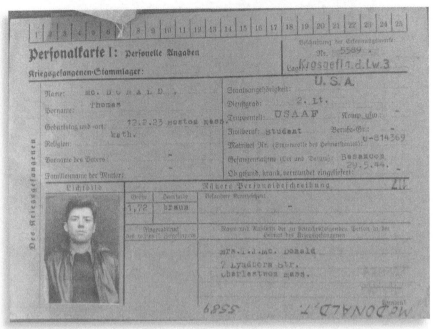

McDonalds POW card

Boring life inside a POW camp

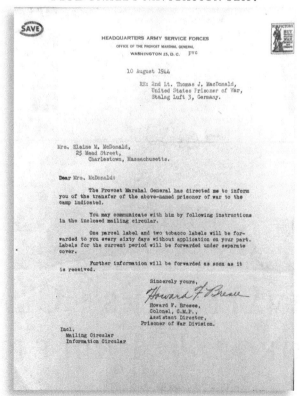

INDIVIDUAL RECORD — COMBAT MISSIONS
COMPLETED

NAME: Thomas J. McDonald   RANK: 2nd Lt.   SERIAL NO. O-841369

QUALIFICATION: Navigator   CREW POSITION: Navigator

MISSION NO.	DATE	TARGET	LENGTH OF MISSION	ENEMY AIRCRAFT LOSSES	REMARKS
1	4/24/44	Friedrichshafen, Ger.	9:15		
2	4/30/44	Clermon Ferrand, Fr.	9:15		
3	5/1/44	Brussels, Belgium	7:00		
4	5/8/44	Berlin, Germany	8:30		
5	5/9/44	Junicourt, France	5:45		
6	5/11/44	Brussels, Belgium	4:55		
7	5/12/44	Brux, Czechoslovakia	9:30		
8	5/25/44	Liege, Belgium	6:50		
9	5/27/44	Strasbourg, Germany	—		Missing In Action
		TOTAL COMBAT TIME	61:00		

McDONALDS NAVIGATION SLIP.

HEADQUARTERS ARMY SERVICE FORCES
OFFICE OF THE PROVOST MARSHAL GENERAL
WASHINGTON 25, D. C.   pvc

10 August 1944

RE: 2nd Lt. Thomas J. MacDonald,
United States Prisoner of War,
Stalag Luft 3, Germany.

Mrs. Elaine M. McDonald,
25 Mead Street,
Charlestown, Massachusetts.

Dear Mrs. McDonald:

The Provost Marshal General has directed me to inform you of the transfer of the above-named prisoner of war to the camp indicated.

You may communicate with him by following instructions in the inclosed mailing circular.

One parcel label and two tobacco labels will be forwarded to you every sixty days without application on your part. Labels for the current period will be forwarded under separate cover.

Further information will be forwarded as soon as it is received.

Sincerely yours,

Howard F. Bresee

Howard F. Bresee,
Colonel, C.M.P.,
Assistant Director,
Prisoner of War Division.

Incl,
Mailing Circular
Information Circular

DETAILS TO MRS. McDONALD ON COMMUNICATING
WITH HER POW HUSBAND.

$\mathcal{B}\,o\,o\,k$ 4

PRIVATE FIRST CLASS
GEORGE J. PELLETIER

Shocked the Whole Nation

George J. Pelletier was born July 18, 1925, in Fitchburg, Massachusetts, where his family lived in their own home on Clyde Street. Pelletier's father was a contractor in Fitchburg and eventually became the city's building inspector. His father was very active in the city, a very popular man. George Pelletier was part of a typically large family in those times; there were three girls and six boys. The Pelletiers were always active in sports, the brothers teaching one another how to play football and baseball during their younger school years. Later, they'd throw in boxing. George's brothers all did well working together in town as contractors in various trades.

When Pearl Harbor was attacked in December 1941, Pelletier was a sixteen-year-old high school student. He said the Pearl Harbor attack "just shocked the whole nation." He added, "We were just stunned that it had occurred. All the fellows in the area that were eighteen and nineteen enlisted right away. Everyone was responding to the crisis. I also had four brothers-in-law that enlisted immediately." Pelletier nodded. "They all did. Everybody did."

Pelletier graduated from Saint Bernard's High School in 1943 and was drafted by the US Army as soon as he turned eighteen years old.

Eager and ready to help, young Pelletier first reported to Fort Devens, Massachusetts, in December 1943. From there, he was whisked to Fort McLellan in Alabama, Fort Jackson in South Carolina, Camp Shelby in Mississippi, Fort Benning in Georgia, and Camp Kilmer in New Jersey to complete his military training—a lot of moving around for this young man.

"Two days after my nineteenth birthday, I was joined with the Eighty-Seventh and we're getting ready to go overseas," said Pelletier. He eventually sailed aboard the *Queen Elizabeth* on October 17, 1944, to Glasgow, Scotland. The men were crowded onto the ship but not uncomfortably, for there was no double loading or sharing of bunk space. Pulling away from the pier at 0630, October 17, the *Queen* sailed from New York Harbor. The sea was calm, the weather clear, and the trip uneventful. The ship was unescorted.[9]

GI vaudeville shows and small bands toured the ship daily. Moving pictures were shown every evening on the blacked-out decks. Card games, men reading or writing letters, or small groups playing phonographs were familiar sights on every deck. Other men just lined the rails and watched the huge waves pushed apart by the speeding bow. Two meals a day were served on the voyage, more than five sittings being required to feed the entire complement of passengers.

After assembling in England on November 12, 1944, the troops moved across the channel to La Havre, France, during the last week of November. By December 6, the Eighty-Seventh had been reassembled near Metz, France.

Pelletier served in Europe as a machine gunner under General George S. Patton's Third Army, M Company, 345th Infantry Regiment, Eighty-Seventh Infantry Division. He witnessed vicious action in France, Belgium, Luxembourg, and Germany. He participated in some of the most barbaric battles during World War II, including those in Ardennes (Battle of the Bulge), Rhineland, and Central Europe, and

---

9 www.87thinfantrydivision.com/history/345th/official/.

the occupation with Russian forces at the German-Czechoslovakian border.[10]

Pelletier was a gunner, and the gunner crew was made up of four soldiers. His job was to shoot the .30-caliber machine gun, from both stationary positions and on the move. It could shoot up to six hundred rounds per minute, or ten rounds per second. The gunner carried the tripod, which weighed fifty-three pounds. Pelletier recalled, "Most of the gunners were big guys. I was 6 feet, 215 pounds, in those days. We had to carry over a hundred pounds. I carried a sidearm .45-caliber pistol and spare shells." The assistant gunner carried the thirty-pound Browning-made gun. His job was also to set the gun into the tripod and feed the belts from the ammo boxes. There was also an ammunition carrier, another soldier who carried all the ammo boxes. Each belt had 250 rounds. Lastly, there was a squad leader. His job was to pick the best spot for setting up the guns and shooting, locating cover to prevent sneak attacks.

THE BATTLE OF THE BULGE

Pelletier was part of many battles, also known as campaigns in the military. One of the most—if not the most—vicious and well documented was known as the Battle of the Bulge. When the Allies jointly invaded Normandy in May 1944, it seemed as though the war might be over soon. The US troops were making ground and hoping Germany would also see the end coming. But even if they did, Adolf Hitler had other plans to try to turn the tide.

Hitler commanded an offensive attack called Operation Watch against American and British forces in the thick, dense forest of Ardennes. The battle was greatly lopsided, with two hundred thousand Germans against eighty thousand Americans. The battle occurred from

---

10 www.lonesentry.com/gi_stories_booklets/87thinfantry/.

December 16, 1944, to January 25, 1945, during one of the worst winters in recent history. Deep snow, strong winds, and difficult terrain made the fighting even more dangerous. Three very powerful German armies were in the forest and rugged mountains of Ardennes. They were trying to break the American line of defense by splitting American forces into two halves and encircling them. The Ardennes Forest extended from Belgium into Luxembourg. The American line was very thin and didn't expect such German forces. At least one entire American division was encircled by the Germans and had to surrender, and more than 6,500 GIs laid down their arms as POWs.[11]

The Germans used GI uniforms on their English-speaking soldiers to sneak into American camps and cause great havoc. They cut communication lines, switched road signs, spread rumors, and created all kinds of problems. Eventually, the Americans caught on and started questioning arriving soldiers about American sporting events and celebrities, and tried other ways to trick the German spies. Those who couldn't answer correctly were usually executed. This was war, after all.

The Germans were having many of their own problems. Fuel, ammunition, and food were no longer easily available for them. Soldiers were malnourished and freezing, and even trucks and tanks were stopped dead in their tracks from fuel starvation. Everything was going wrong for both sides. From insufficient clothing, causing frozen feet and bodies, to poor commands, communications, supplies, and the weather, it was a brutal experience for all involved.

Not until the skies cleared enough for US aircraft to finally drop supplies did the Allies regain control of the forest. The Germans really threw everything they had at the Allies. This was to be a big win for the Germans and substantial loss for the Allies, working into the morale for both sides.

---

11 https://en.m.wikipedia.org/wiki/Battle_of_the_Bulge.

Both sides paid a heavy price for every inch of ground they could recover. The battle raged on for three consecutive days until Allied forces joined the desperate Americans and kept the Germans from breaking through the lines. They continued an incredible battle—one never seen before or since. The powerful German army had created a sixty-mile bulge in the defense. But the cost was staggering. For the irreparable German Army, the end would soon follow.

More than a million men fought for this important forest and it's moral implications for the winners in eastern Belgium and northern Luxembourg. Initially, the American and British troops were outnumbered eighty-three thousand to two hundred thousand. Eventually, the numbers of troops were raised on both sides to the following levels:

- More than 610,000 Americans, using three armies and six corps.
- More than 55,000 British, using three divisions plus French troops.
- More than 72,000 Free French.
- More than 500,000 Germans, using three armies and ten corps.

Casualties were high.

- 89,500 Americans (19,000 killed, 47,500 wounded, 23,000 captured or missing)
- 1,408 British (200 killed, 969 wounded, 239 missing)
- 125,000 Germans (killed, wounded, missing or captured)
- 3,000 civilians

More than eight hundred tanks were lost on each side, and approximately a thousand aircraft were destroyed. It was a major and destructive battle and one of the bloodiest in all of World War II.[12]

---

12 https://en.m.wikipedia.org/wiki/Battle_of_the_Bulge.

"Food was a problem," said Pelletier, seven decades later. "We did have K rations. Toughest part of the Bulge was that we had to sleep outside. Each guy carried half a tent, moved some snow, put down blankets, and made do." Pelletier, however, never made mention of the pain he must have endured. He must have suffered from having frozen feet, hearing problems, severe back pain, and more for the rest of his life.

The Siegfried Line was an actual line of defense. Large concrete pyramid-looking pillars were set just far enough apart to prevent tanks and vehicles from moving past them. The line was stretched more than 390 miles, with more than eighteen thousand bunkers, tunnels, and tank traps. It was planned beginning in 1936 and built between 1938 and 1940.[13]

In all, Pelletier's Eighty-Seventh Infantry Division spent 154 days of action in the European theater of operations, from December 6, 1944, to May 8, 1945, when Germany unconditionally surrendered.

---

13 https://en.m.wikipedia.org/wiki/Siegfried_Line.

Midnight Sneak across the Rhine River

A s mentioned earlier, Pelletier's brothers taught him various sports and even the martial art/combat sport of boxing. They put him in a ring and charged ten cents to watch the boxing matches. It helped a little when he was drafted; he boxed three matches while in the service. He won his first match in the first round. "Bloody nose for the other guy, and that stopped it," he recalled. The second one was a little tougher, but he won in a decision by the judges. "The third guy was a real boxer," Pelletier said. "*Oh shit,* I said to myself, and just plowed into him right away. The real boxer got a bloody nose and that was the end of him!" Pelletier went three bouts and retired undefeated.

Pelletier was fluent in French and translated for executive officers when asked. Although he wasn't called upon often, he was proud of his ability to help out as a translator—another one of his many talents.

They pushed across Europe until the end of the war, and Pelletier recalled being among the first Americans to cross the Rhine River in Germany, where they advanced forward to the Czech border before receiving orders to come home.

Pelletier was among the first two hundred men to cross the Rhine River; they sneaked across at midnight, having been specifically trained for the mission. "They took us to a pond, and we were gonna have a cookout. There were boats out there. 'Go out and have a good time on the boats,' they told us. Once they called us all together, they said, 'We hope you liked those boats 'cause that's what you're gonna use when you cross the Rhine.'" Several other regiments were faking a crossing to get the Germans' attention while Pelletier's troops conducted the real crossing.

"It was a very quiet, moonless night; it was midnight and we started to cross," Pelletier said. "I was assigned to a heavy-weapons company, a rifle company. We had to tape our gear to us and be very quiet—no talking, nothing. I was in the second wave. We snuck across the river, and within one hour, we had our whole battalion over without losing a man—not a shot fired. We caught them all in their holes before we took and secured the high ground."

Daybreak allowed the Americans to cross the river using a specially designed pontoon bridge. Trucks, tanks, and troops all filed across peacefully. "The engineers that developed those plans were great," said Pelletier.

Chapter 3

His Letter, His Story, Their Life

Following is a letter from George to his girlfriend and soon-to-be wife, Cecile Poitras. It has been copied as written to capture all his details and emotion, and has been edited only slightly for clarity and style.

Schlesinger, Germany

May 24, 1945

Dearest Cecile,

Hello, Sweetheart, it's me again ready to write a letter I've never written at all before. Yep, censorship is over except base censor and we can write about all that happened. So now prepare to hear my autobiography. It's about 1 PM here in the afternoon; it's been raining all day so I'm going to write most of the afternoon because I go on guard tonight and tomorrow.

Paragraph 1, section 1 (ahem)

I left Ft. Jackson sometime around three or four of October, boarded the train, and lo and behold landed at Camp Kilmer, New Jersey, not far from home. We remain there a few days, had some swell chow there, issued equipment, etc. Then boarded the train late at night headed for New York Harbor. Then boarded none other than the *Queen Elizabeth* herself, the largest vessel afloat. This all happened on October 16, I believe.

We sailed at the break of dawn on the 17th, everything was swell, weather and all except that we were mighty crowded. As Bob would say, we [were] like sardines in a can and you couldn't twitch an eyelid without tickling the next guy. On the boat we played cards after and read. I stood on top deck quite often, watching passing vessels and convoys. We zigzagged often and changed our course often in order to shake off any pursuing submarine. Rumors had it that a submarine was on our tail but I doubt it. Anyhow we had nice weather on the whole trip but many of the boys were sick. I was rather fortunate however and remained quite healthy.

After being at sea 6 days we [were] near the coast of Ireland [and] were able to see a lot of Ireland. We then continued on until we came to Greenwich, Scotland. I was amazed at the number of war vessels there. All types of battleships to submarines. The next day we disembarked and were [ferried] to shore. There a train was waiting for us and the Red Cross with coffee and doughnuts.

Soon the train pulled out [and] we traveled to Scotland and a good part of England before we stopped at Leek, England. Leek is where we remained after one month. It is there where we played all kinds of sports, received our first mail, drilled, and received our passes to nearby cities. Soon after Thanksgiving we took a train from Southampton. From there we boarded an English boat, which took us across the channel to the port of LeHavre in France. Soon after, landing trucks appeared and took us for a long journey somewhere in France. Exactly where, I don't know. Here we remained for over a week in this marshaling area. It was miserable as we slept in mud, walked in mud; anyway everything was rain and mud.

Soon we received our first mission. So we boarded aboard cattle cars and took off. Our mission was to take the remaining forts occupied by Germans and Metz, France. We were not there long before they all gave up. In the meantime two other regiments of our division were in action in the Saar, this all happening around 5th of December.

Now we took off for the Saar and were ready for action the next day. However, it wasn't 24 hours before we jumped off. I will never forget it. The [Heinies] spotted us coming around the hill and started picking us off. Shells were landing everywhere as close as 5 yards from me. I was dazed but prayed like mad. I then spotted a hole in the ground, which probably saved my life, as three men behind me were hit. We took a beating that day. We dug in that night under fire. At 4 the next morning we took off or jumped off into the attack once again minus anything to eat or drink and minus sleep. That day we advanced 5 miles into the woods, flanking our objective, while other companies came in on the other sides. Again we were shelled continuously, one of my buddies was killed, two more wounded, all in my platoon. Soon we ran out of ammunition, had no water or food. There we dug in for two days hoping that Jerry didn't see us, in the meantime one platoon of I Company [to] which we were attached started back for what we needed.

We were 3 days without food or water, our squad or rather what was left four out of seven drank water from the water jacket of our gun. Incidentally I'm still a machine gunner. I was assistant gunner at the time. But 18 hours later we heard our platoon coming back with rations and water. Soon after that we were relieved by another battalion. Whew, what a relief. They continued on the attack while we drew back a mile or so, dug in, and rested up for 2 days.

We lost a lot of men here; it was rough. Then we pulled out again to dig in and hold our lines while divisions on our right and left caught up to us. Now the bulge started and we transferred from the Seventh Army to the Third. Then we took off for the bulge, a day later we jumped off into the attack and drove the Jerry back after he had counterattacked on New Year's Eve. We lost more of our buddies here out of my platoon, again I escaped. We took a major part in the bulge and were successful. It was rough in the Ardennes Forest attacking in the snow, digging in and sleeping there but we came out OK still pounding the [Heinies'] back.

The bulge being nearly over we took off for Luxembourg. There we felt the Jerry out for a week, trying to find out what he had across the river. Now we were relieved by [a] new division and sent back into what was left of the bulge. We jumped off again to town after town and drove into Germany, being under constant fire of Jerry. Lost a few men.

Now came the hard part, cracking the Siegfried Line. Our battalion spearheaded this drive and we pushed on. It was rough, we were shelled and fired upon continuously. We lost more men here. Our Second Platoon [was] practically wiped out. Our platoon lost a few men. Our squad was still in fair shape. Sergeant Paul DeVeccho, Frank and I, and Chuck Kovinsky were left. Here Paul was put in for the Silver Star for dragging "Red," a kid in our squad, to safety after he was hit. Frank and I had many close ones again but escaped. Others weren't as fortunate.

Now came the town I despise, Neundorf. We captured it one day only after a bitter scrap. Here Frank was wounded and I became First Gunner. We remained there about six days dug in and held. Jerry was determined to recapture the town and counterattacked. At the time they counterattacked, our squad was up on a hill in a patch of woods with a handful of riflemen. That night we went through hell. We lost communications, were nearly surrounded, and [were] shelled all night by theirs and our artillery. The next morning we were relieved, thank God, and went back a couple of miles for a few days' rest. This was in February. Then we came back to Neundorf to relieve the 346th, who had relieved us. Every day we were sniped at, shelled daily all the time. They hit the room we were in several times.

Soon, we jumped off again to take the next town, by name, Ruth. We took it after quite a scrap, lost a lot of men. I was scared stiff as we advanced through a minefield. There I saw men get blown to bits, what a sight, no one to help them. After we took this town we had Jerry in the run, so we kept after him. Boarded tanks and T.D.'s and took off after them until we drove all the way through close to the Rhine.

Then came out on mission, assault the Moselle River and take Coblenz. That we did. We assaulted the Rhine and fought street after street to take the city. We had quite a time of it. Here Paul was shot by a sniper, again I got out OK. Frank took over again. I forgot to mention Frank came back to us. So now I became First Gunner again. Frank is now squad leader and sergeant. Well, anyway, we took Coblenz; another friend of mine was killed and others [were] wounded. Hey, we stayed for a few days, had movies, drank nothing else but champagne (ahem). Big shots, you know, high class as anything.

Now came the Rhine, so we moved a little further south near the banks of the Rhine, where we practiced in small boats in order to be ready for the Rhine. Then came the hour we were to go. We really sweated out, as we knew what would happen should they catch us on the river.

Under cover of darkness we shoved off. K Company was on the first wave; we were attached to them with our four heavy machine guns. We took off on the second wave, nothing happened. K Company got across unnoticed; however, we were spotted in the middle of the river. They opened up with a machine gun, but it was silenced. Then 20 mm flak started lobbing over our heads, so we paddled like mad. We had a lot of new boys with us and they were a problem. All kids, fresh replacements without enough experience. Well, we got over OK and I was the first man from M Company to hit the opposite shore of the Rhine. From then on to where we are now we lost but few men drove fast and hard across Germany until the war's end. The day the war ended we jumped off to clear roadblocks. So here I was, the war was over, and I was OK. I [thanked] the Lord that day.

I failed to mention 75 percent of what happened between December 5 and May 12 but this will give you a better idea of what I've been doing and how fortunate I was. I probably could be a sergeant today, but I refused to do so at Coblenz where we lost a lot of men. I figured I was OK at First Gunner without much responsibility. My job is not only being first gunner but assistant squad leader. At times I've been Acting Squad Leader.

So the boys I came over with in my platoon aren't coming back. Out of 36 we lost a lot. There are 15 original men left, half of them with the Purple Heart. So you see I was lucky, one of the few never wounded. A lot of the boys have won decorations. We lost 3 platoon leaders. And Sergeant Johnny, my section leader when we first started, won his commission on the battlefield and is now a 2nd Lieut. He also holds the Silver Star. He's quite a boy and only 21 years old. We are the youngest outfit of any army, by the way, and we have an excellent record. Our battalion made up of J.K.L. & M. companies boasts the best record in the best Bn. and C.O. We took every objective, captured many Jerrys, never lost an inch of ground, have been counterattacked but never set back. No enemy patrols have ever penetrated our lines. Our C.O. says the only thing we failed to do was to drink up all the champagne in Coblenz.

All through this I've learned to realize a lot of things. I know what war is now. I've seen it, I've seen men die and maimed for life. I've seen homes destroyed, families all separated, poor, unfed little children. Now when I get back home I know what needs to be done and no one is to cross me or any other of these G.I.s who know all this. We owe a debt to our buddies and we're going to see that what they wanted and dreamed about is accomplished.

Well, darling, I don't know whether I should have mentioned all this, but I know it's all over now and I'm OK so I've told you some things that have happened since I left the States. I don't think I'll tell you anymore, the rest shouldn't be told, I guess. So we will forget it. I owe a lot to you, Cecile, to my family and all who prayed for me, [kept] writing me and gave me encouragement when it was needed. Honestly many times you letters done a lot of things that no one else could ever do.

Well, Cecile, I'll sign off now. This has been rather a long letter. In the meantime please don't worry, I'm OK, hoping to see you soon. Got to knock off now and get a few things straightened out. I will try and write tomorrow, I'm on guard.

Oh say, can you tell the family what I told you in this letter because I don't plan on writing it all over again. So you can show them the rest of the pages if you wish too. Hope everything is OK with you and the family. So long for now, God Bless you, I love you as much as ever, Cecile, and miss you.

All my love,

George

Chapter 4

His Journey with Life Changes

H ere's an excerpt following Pelletier's journey from the booklet *Stalwart and Strong*, which covers the history of the Eighty-Seventh Infantry Division to which Pelletier was assigned. This story was one published by *The Stars and Stripes* in Paris in 1944–1945:

> The story of the 87th Infantry Division's participation in the European phase of World War II. The vicious baptism in the Saar, the snow-mantled hills and icy forests of the Ardennes. The Luxembourg defense, the flaming rupture of the Siegfried Line, the Kyll and Ahr. The smoothly executed Moselle crossing and the capture of historic Koblenz, the brilliant forced passage of the Rhine, the irresistible surge eastward across Germany to the borders of Czechoslovakia.

Pelletier remembered patrolling in a jeep, big machine gun at the ready, to meet up with some Czech troops at their border. He enjoyed the camaraderie with Allied troops. By this time, it was clear that Hitler's Third Reich had endured enough war. "There were entire units surrendering to us. None of them were armed," he recalled.

Coincidentally, Pelletier was on the first division to return home. They were sent home on a leave, expected to head south to train for a major invasion of Japan. Fortunately, the war ended while they were Stateside. Instead, he was sent to Fort Devens. George Pelletier ended his military service with an honorable discharge on May 1, 1946.

Two months after he returned home, George and Cecile were married. It was time to start a life and not dwell on the horrors of the past. Eventually, they bought a small home in Fitchburg that was literally being moved. The house was rolled down the street about a quarter mile on telephone poles and placed onto an existing foundation. They raised their family in that home and still live there.

Pelletier never smoked cigarettes. "The guys would tell me, 'It won't do you any good [to not smoke].'" He shrugged. "Well, I'm still here and they're all gone. ... I used to run two miles, five days a week—bicycles, treadmills, all the time. I did that for forty-one years." Years of physical conditioning made Pelletier a regular at the YMCA, where he kept as fit as possible.

After the war, Pelletier worked for the Fallulah Paper Company, like so many of his friends and relatives. The paper mills' constant contamination of the Nashua River led to laws that eventually limited their production, and Pelletier found himself looking elsewhere for employment. In 1958, he attended the FBI National Academy in Boston. In 1960, he was appointed to the Fitchburg Police Department to protect and serve Americans—not surprising.

He was assigned the position of juvenile police officer, helping to keep the town's youngsters in line. He then went to Boston for schooling and became the police department's traffic manager. He's proud that he was able to help the department receive federal grants for cruisers and other items they needed. At one meeting with a local firearms manufacturer, Pelletier made a deal and traded in all the old firearms for all new revolvers for the entire department. He was making a good name for himself with the chief and was proud of his accomplishments. He talked about his time as a policeman and being able to make a difference in other people's lives. As an example, he once brought in the families of some kids instead of arresting them. He gave the whole group a pep talk about being grown up and doing the right things, and was pleased to see them take his words seriously. He never had any trouble with them again. Once again, this gave the chief confidence in Pelletier's judgment.

Years later, after being in constant pain, Pelletier went to have his back examined. The doctor reviewed his MRI and said two discs had compound fractures and discs four and five were herniated. He was then sent to another VA doctor, who noticed he was wearing hearing aids. As his hearing was at 60 percent, the doctor asked him what he had done in the war and Pelletier simply answered, "Machine gunner." His feet had frozen during the Battle of the Bulge. When we visited, he casually mentioned having had three cancerous spots removed from his right leg. He's just an amazing man, taking life as it comes.

He was a member of the Veterans of the Battle of the Bulge group. "Those who fought it will never forget it. The VBOB was organized to make certain that it would never be forgotten," read a letter from Central Massachusetts Chapter 22. "Had some nice reunions," Pelletier said, "but that stopped about ten years ago. They all died off."

Following is a poem about the horrors and pain of the Battle of the Bulge, written by F. S. "Slim" Lychock, Company F, Second Battalion, 328th Infantry, Twenty-Sixth Infantry Division, while in a hospital in 1946. It is reprinted from page 10 of *The Bulge Bugle*, Volume VI, Number 4, November 1987.[14]

Dogface

Cold mud. Piercing rain. Hours marching. No rest.
Shouldered rifle, bandoliers, grenades across his breast.

---

14 www.veteransofthebattleofthebulge.org.

Feet wet and sore. Mind weary. His heart sick. Cast to hell those misery did inflict.

Night his blanket. The muddy earth his home. His body shivers. His heart weeps. Lips give no moan. He looks up to God and asks, when will it end? The makers of this evil. Their day in hell to spend. Morning comes.

The enemy is near. Hell. He's here! Body cold and sore. Brain alert. A heart in fear. Cracking of rifles. The demonish screech of a shell. The sight of blood. A call for aid. The brink of hell. The battle rages.

Pain. Blood. And death heroically prevail. Victory comes. Hope of sleep. Something to eat. Perhaps, some mail. Day never ceasing in sacrifice. Misery and pain. Will it ever end? Will life ever be sane again?

Chapter 5

Home, Marriage, Family, and Being Sane Again

George Pelletier and Cecile Poitras met at the American Type Foundry before the war. "She was a beautiful lady," said Pelletier. They married two months after the war ended and had five boys and three girls. As the saying goes, the apple doesn't fall far from the tree. Eldest son John retired as a captain from the US Army and Jim from the US Air Force. Tony did two terms in Vietnam, and the two youngest boys, Mark and Peter, worked as partners for years, making a thriving local general contracting business. The girls' accomplishments have been amazing as well. Carol and Linda are both in the medical field, and Susan works with young preschool children. Not surprisingly, George and Cecile have had a positive influence on their children's professional choices.

"They have done well—very proud of them," George said of his grown children. During my first visit with him, a few of his sons were there in the yard, talking—they're never too far away if needed. During another visit, Susan stopped by just to check in on her dad.

A common family theme with that generation also came from Pelletier. "In those days, we were very family oriented," he said. "Families were close. Our parents were very strict with us, going to school, getting your education. And religion—we were very churchgoing people. I had a sister who was a nun, cousins who were nuns or priests."

George J. Pelletier was awarded the Combat Infantry Badge, Bronze Star with Oak Leaf Cluster, Good Conduct Medal, American Campaign Medal, European-African Middle-Eastern Campaign Medal, WWII Victory Medal, Army of Occupation Medal, three battle stars, and the Honorable Service Lapel Button WWII.

He has carried these journeys and events with him throughout his life. Pelletier extended his war experience from being an average eighteen-year-old kid to his candidacy at FBI National Academy Associates, Quantico, Virginia, to the Fitchburg Police Department. In July 1987, he retired as a sergeant from the Fitchburg Police Department after thirty-eight years of honorable service.

Your lifelong service to our country is admirable and very much appreciated. Thank you, sir.

PELLETIER AND HIS MOM

PELLETIER READY FOR SERVICE.

GERMANY, APRIL 1, 1945

THE SIEGFRIED LINE

"Dragon's Teeth."

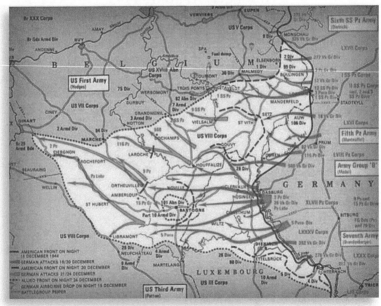

Battle of the Bulge

PELLETIER'S BRONZE STAR AWARD.

Book 5

TECHNICIAN FIFTH GRADE CORPORAL CHARLES M. SANDERSON

Chapter 7

Never Forgetting the Powerful Howitzer

Charlie Sanderson was born in Shirley, Massachusetts, on March 19, 1925. He was ninety years old at the time of this interview. His mind and memory are sharper than even he'd admit to—another humble veteran. His parents were born in town as well. We sat on a white wooden farmer's porch, where Sanderson, now living on many acres the next town over in Lunenburg, Massachusetts, was looking out over his field. It was a cool May morning when we talked, and he reminisced about things not discussed in many years but not forgotten either. In a home on some of the land that was part of a land grant many decades ago between his ancestors and the local American Indians, Charlie and his wife, Marguerite, live happily on many quiet acres in the small town with just over ten thousand neighbors.

Sanderson has one brother six years his elder. Sanderson also has two sons and two daughters: Robert, Richard, Maryanne, and Susan.

He attended Shirley Grammar School and Leominster High School, but like many during those times, he didn't graduate from high school. He was, however, drafted into the United States Army in 1943 at the age of eighteen. The army recruiter asked him if he liked guns, he said yes because he grew up shooting them. "I didn't know the difference between a rifle and a gun and a weapon, but I learned,"

Sanderson recalled. "The outfit I was in was with guns. A gun is like a Howitzer. It can shoot and lob them in over a mountain. A rifle gun has to shoot direct." A Howitzer can shoot twenty miles, either directly or over a mountaintop.

Sanderson started his basic training for the military in Fort Bragg, North Carolina. He remembered going for a walk by himself "to check out the other units." He saw a barbershop. "Just for the hell of it, I walked into the barbershop. My barber from Shirley was doing barber work, cutting GIs' hair, and he was there," Sanderson said, amazed at the coincidence.

Unlike most soldiers who finished their training and were selected to be shipped overseas, Sanderson was rushed over as a replacement and completed his basic training in Salisbury Plains, England, near the white cliffs of Dover—not a pleasant or safe place to be in early 1944.

Sanderson was now official property of the US First Army, 552nd Field Artillery Battalion, Seventy-Eighth Infantry Division, AAA Automatic Weapons Battalion under Major General Edwin P. Parker.

He was placed in a combat troop and was off in an LST (landing ship, tank), heading for the shores of Normandy before he knew what had hit him—soon after the initial invasion of June 6, 1944. Sanderson's rank was a corporal technician fifth grade, with two stripes with a *T* on his sleeve, as a truck driver. He would be addressed as Tech Corporal. However, like everyone else, he played many other roles during the war.

Operation Overlord—D-day+

S anderson eventually landed on Omaha Beach in Normandy, France. At that time, the Allies were only two miles inland, just about a week after the initial D-day invasion. His LST, which was designed to carry troops, supplies, and tanks across the water, was one of the first unloaded. Each LST had two or three trucks in it; the soldiers each carried half of a large gun as well as a carbine rifle, gas mask, and a few other needed supplies.[15]

Sanderson had more than just the German Army to worry about. Another enemy was also waiting for him—water. Sanderson was worried because he had never learned how to swim. The water looked deep, the waves were crashing over the sides, the ship was rocking, and he was overloaded with weight like the rest of the troops. Charlie Sanderson, less than twenty years old, didn't know how to swim in an amphibious monster being dumped in vicious enemy territory, where it would be shot at and bombed. The Germans had various defenses on the beach, some similar to the Siegfried Line with six-foot-square concrete blocks staggered so you couldn't drive a truck or tank between them, barbed wire, metal blockades, and plenty of mines. Those were the passive obstructions; the active ones were the Third Reich's fortified troops

---

15 https://en.m.wikipedia.org/wiki/Landing_Ship,_Tank.

shelling and bombing from above the beaches. Two miles back wasn't very far for wartime fighting.

Barrage balloons were everywhere, their thick steel cables hanging down. The cables were intended to prevent aircraft from being able to fly low on their strafing runs. The aircraft unloaded thousands of rounds of gunfire as they flew low passes over the Allies, making headway up the beaches and onward. The balloons could go as high as ten thousand feet if needed, although they were used at a much lower level for this operation.

"Come in during high tide like a sitting duck, drop your ramp down, they yelled, 'Sanderson, get your truck out … Go, go!'" Sanderson remembered. He was afraid, because he couldn't swim. He also needed to know how deep the water was so the LST wouldn't just flip over once the front gate was opened. He stuck a ten-foot-long stick into the water to gauge the depth and found the stick was not long enough.

"I can't go! I can't go!" he screamed. "It'll stand on its nose."

But they were yelling at him, "Go, go!"

Again, he said, "It can't go. It'll stand on its nose. I don't want to drive the friggin' truck over and tip it over. That'll be the end of everything."

They had to wait for the tide to come back out, playing sitting ducks again—strafing and shelling coming at them the whole time. They were unfortunate because, unbeknownst to them at first, they had stopped in a shell crater. That's why the water was so deep around them where they'd stopped.

"The Germans didn't know we were coming, but they were real smart. They were preparing for this for years," Sanderson explained. "They'd have a swamp, for instance, and in it they had posts everywhere about ten feet high, knowing that someday gliders would be trying to invade and the gliders would crash into them. They were everywhere."

Recalling his sights on the Normandy landing, he said, "When we came onto land, there were dead Germans and Americans everywhere. I noticed that the American officer had a one-inch white bar, three inches high, on the front and back of his helmet. Commissioned officers bars were going vertically, the noncommissioned officers were going horizontally. The Germans would use that as a target. You'd see the helmet with brains in it and busted open. You'd see the Red Cross on their arm, giving intravenous [treatments], and you'd see them both laying there, dead. They didn't recognize Red Cross."

The Allies also used many glider aircraft to fly and land behind enemy territory to supply the anticipated incoming troops. "You'd see silk parachutes everywhere. When they released gliders, some would have cannons in them or jeeps. They'd release them at night. The gliders crash-landed wherever they fell to earth. Some of them survived and got together with a jeep or something. It was a disaster."

To quote General William C. Westmoreland, US Army, regarding the gliders, "They were the only aviators during World War II who had no motors, no parachutes, and no second chances."[16]

"Aircraft started coming over, so many bombers coming over," Sanderson said. "It would have been a nice, sunny day. Within two hours, it was hazy and dark from the smoke, dust, and whatever. So many would come and drop their bombs and head back. I honestly thought they were going back and refueling and coming back. They just couldn't have had that many bombers coming in like that. It was just unbelievable—seemed like there was no end in sight to it. The sky was full of flak everywhere. You could hear the bombing, see a wing fly off or a tail fly off. It was dumbfounding, knowing those people were up there doing that and there wasn't a damn thing those on the ground could do but just keep going. Just sitting ducks, like, ya know?"

---

16 https://en.m.wikipedia.org/wiki/American_airborne_landings_in_Normandy.

Chapter 3

The Gun Would Get So Hot
You Could Fry an Egg on It

Moving forward into Normandy and other parts of France, the troops fired on the towns of Saint-Lô and Sainte-Mère-Église. "Return fire was nonstop. Everything was coming at us." Just because Allied troops had a large gun that could shoot twenty miles didn't mean they sat waiting and shooting from afar. The idea was to push the Germans back and move the Allies forward. They'd go right up to the "pack 75s," smaller, more portable Howitzer guns, generally located ahead on the front lines.

"One time, I looked up over the hill and saw all the tanks lined up," Sanderson said. "I thought they were American tanks. They were Germans and they started firing at us. We were laying out a position and didn't know we had gone too far." The land between the two fighting sides is known as no-man's-land. Sanderson's troop had gone too far into German-occupied territory; they had to get out of there in a hurry.

Again, Sanderson was part of the 552nd Field Artillery Battalion. They had three gun batteries: A, B, and C Battery. Their weapon was the enormous, American-made 240 mm Howitzer Cannon that would shoot a 365-pound projectile within a twenty-mile range, using eighty-five pounds of gunpowder per shot. This big weapon of war could also be moved around as needed to advance.

Once a position was established and laid out, Sanderson began to empty his truck for action. He took a big canvas and put it down exactly where the massive Howitzer gun was to be located. The canvas had holes in it with metal grommets, and it took three men to lay it out. Assigned to a twenty-one-man crew, Sanderson was up front first. They'd put the large steel spades attached to the sides of the gun into the ground for support, but needed large enough holes to accommodate the recoil based on the gun's nose's aim. When the other part of his crew showed up, all they had to do was start digging. After that, they placed "a thousand sandbags around it," Sanderson said. "Sometimes you had soft or sandy soil to work with."

They used prime movers to move the Howitzers around—not a tank. A prime mover is a specialized heavy-duty gun tractor used to tow artillery pieces of various weight and sizes. They took two prime movers and put them at 45 degrees on either side of the Howitzer, cabling the gun to them for further stability.

Each man had his own job. A gunner would sit on a metal seat on one side of the gun and did quadrant lateral settings. Another sat on the other side, configuring the elevation settings. The two spun the big steering wheels for accuracy. When ready, the gunner got on a phone with the commander and yelled, "Set," then "Ready" and the commander on the other end of the line would tell them when to fire. To work just the gun, "There would be two men on the gun; seven on ram-staff and four to bring the projectile out."

With seven men on the ram-staff, a twelve-foot manual push rod got the projectile into the gun. "They'd yell, 'One, two, three ... ram!' and slam the 365-pound bullet into the barrel of the Howitzer. It all went as fast as you could go ... to have a round in the air every minute."

There was a sergeant in charge of maintenance for all this equipment. The prime movers were all covered in camouflage to hide from reconnaissance planes. "The noise was tough," explained Sanderson. "You were supposed to stand on your toes, open your mouth, and block your ears. How you gonna do that when you had to measure the recoil on the gun? The gun would recoil sixty-five inches," he remembered. "The hotter the gun got from firing, the farther back the gun would recoil.[17]

"We needed cooks, truck drivers, mechanics, and others soldiers' efforts of the unit to make it all work. Some of the others would be guarding the trucks and facilities during the shooting. You had guard duty, two on and four off, and sometimes we'd agree to four on and two off to give more people a break or [to] sleep more at night. But you had to be close to your gun. Your pup tent was very close by the gun. When they called a fire mission, you had to be quickly available. Or, if there was a fire mission and you were sleeping ... well, at least trying to sleep during all of that."

Further inquiry about his crew continued. "The sergeant is like the head mechanic; he knows what's to happen and when to move on. Everything is camouflaged and ready to go when needed. They all carried the carbine rifles with a sling over their shoulders." He shook his head. "Nobody could believe what it was like."

In front of the guns was a six-foot pile of loose grass or dirt caused by a vacuum from the firing. "One time," Sanderson recalled with a smile, "there was a half dozen sheep close by. We fired over them and there was a whole pile of loose wool in front of the gun. It didn't pull it out of them, but loose wool from their bodies was in with the grass. It was kind of funny."

The food was mostly K rations. The only time their cook was able to provide decent meals was when they got into a quiet zone where they

---

17 https://en.m.wikipedia.org/wiki/240_mm_howitzer_M1#.

could kind of lie back, with not much going on. They sometimes took the big kettles, which looked like metal garbage cans, and set four of them out. They then took extra gunpowder bags and threw them onto a fire—which got the water boiling in just a couple of minutes. They threw C rations into the water so they could have hot food. But most of the time, it was K rations. The benefits of K rations were for quick eating meals and maximum energy while C rations were more for sustained daily food intake.

K rations were individual portions of canned combat food and provided breakfast, lunch, and supper. According to Wikipedia, a day's menu consisted of the following:

Breakfast Unit: canned entree (chopped ham and eggs, veal loaf), biscuits, a dried fruit bar or cereal bar, Halazone water purification tablets, a four-pack of cigarettes, chewing gum, instant coffee, and sugar (granulated, cubed, or compressed).

Dinner Unit: canned entree (processed cheese, ham, or ham and cheese), biscuits, fifteen malted-milk tablets (in early versions) or five caramels (in later versions), sugar (granulated, cubed, or compressed), a salt packet, a four-pack of cigarettes and a box of matches, chewing gum, and a powdered-beverage packet (lemon [c. 1940], orange [c. 1943], or grape [c. 1945] flavor).

Supper Unit: canned meat, consisting of chicken paté, pork luncheon meat with carrot and apple (first issue), beef and pork loaf (second issue), or sausages; biscuits; a 2-ounce D ration emergency chocolate bar, tropical-formula bar, or (in temperate climates) commercial sweet chocolate bar; a packet of toilet paper tissues; a four-pack of cigarettes; chewing gum, and a bouillon soup cube or powder packet.

In total, the three meals provided between 2,830 and 3,000 calories, depending upon their components. As it was originally intended as an "assault" ration to be issued for short durations, the K ration was designed to be used for a maximum of fifteen meals. The K ration was produced by the Cracker Jack Company with a waxed-paper ration box, about the same size as the company's famous Cracker Jack box.

The Type C ration consisted of a one-pound meat unit (M-unit) of 12 ounces (340 g). In the initial Type C ration, there were only three variations of the main course: meat and beans, meat and potato hash, or meat and vegetable stew. Also issued was one bread-and-dessert can, or B-unit. Each daily ration (that is, enough food for one soldier for one day) consisted of six twelve-ounce (340 g) cans (three M-units and three B-units), and an individual meal consisted of one M-unit and one B-unit. The original oblong can was replaced with the more common cylindrical design in June 1939 because of mass production problems with the former can shape.[18]

18 http://en.wikipedia.org/wiki/C-ration
http://en.wikipedia.org/wiki/K_ration.

Chapter 4

The Red Ball Express

After the initial invasion of Normandy was successful, it started to turn into a stalemate in which neither side was advancing or retreating. Information about the hedgerows in Normandy and the fighting there has been well documented. The Allies decided on a massive aerial attack code named Operation Cobra commencing on July 25, 1944. By July 27, the German Army was finally becoming scattered and disorganized. The results were outstanding and allowed the Allies to push east faster than they had planned. As a result, supplies, food, ammunition, and other items were needed to be sent to the front lines as expeditiously as possible.

The Red Ball Express was conceived in a thirty-six-hour brainstorming session. It lasted only three months from August to November 1944. Without it, the campaign in the European theater could have dragged on for years. At the peak of its operation, the Red Ball Express was running 5,938 vehicles, carrying 12,342 tons of supplies to forward depots daily.

The logistics are staggering when running a world war. An American infantry division required 150 tons of gasoline per day, and an armored division 350 tons per day. Some of the supply lines were miles and miles long, and the amount of provisions and munitions numbered thousands of tons. This was almost ten times that of World War I.[19]

Sanderson was part of the Red Ball Express during its entire duration. "They painted a ten-inch red ball on the passenger side window of the truck [he was driving]. We were pushing the Germans across France so fast, we couldn't keep up with supplies. You hauled, but never knew what it was going to be ... ammunition, gasoline, or food. When you're in convoy, you can't break convoy. You stay and you can't pull out. One of my schoolmates was sitting on the side of the road ... with some of his guys and a vehicle ... and I'm going along, and I couldn't stop to see him," Sanderson recalled, shaking his head at the memory.

Sanderson shared some of his memories of the Battle of the Bulge: "During the Battle of the Bulge, the Germans spearheaded around us. We were in the middle, and they had us surrounded. The lieutenant told us, 'We're going to fight until the last man. The first man to turn around, I'll shoot him in the back.' That's what the lieutenant told us. Blood and Guts, General Patton, came in with his tanks. When he came by, you could see those tanks rolling around. He saved our ass, you know. We were surrounded." When asked if he'd ever met General Patton, Sanderson responded with a smile. "I drove past him once. I knew who he was, but he didn't know who I was."

From a distant memory, Sanderson remembered another interesting story, detailing what the Ardennes Forest looked like. "Did you ever see land when a tornado's come through? Did you ever see trees and stuff, twisted and broken off? The whole friggin' forest was like that. I drove down a road and there were horses hooked to cannons—German horse-drawn artillery. Our men came down through and strafed them. We just had to push them off the road so we could get through. Imagine that—using horse-drawn artillery in World War II. Everything the

---

19 http://www.transchool.lee.army.mil/museum/transportation%20museum/ redballintro.htm.

Germans had, they used. That was the Ardennes Forest." Sanderson was stunned to see the once-mighty Third Reich reduced to using horse-drawn artillery.

"They called them battles, but to me it was a battle all the way through.

"I often thought that our captain didn't do things fairly. I may be wrong, but I was a truck driver. I was picked out every time a special detail came up or something. Any time the army wanted a truck from this outfit or that outfit without interfering ... I was picked from my outfit. I had to go further back and pick up a German cannon. Me and my assistant driver [coincidentally, Tommy O'Dea from Waltham, Massachusetts, was his assistant driver], we had to go back and get German cannons," he said, still amazed. "There were three trucks chosen. We set up by the river to harass the Germans, so they'd think we were all over here, but it was just the three of us. Of course, we'd take return artillery. They were firing on us and we were just firing at will—no targets or nothing. We'd just fire the friggin' things at will. Load them up and fire them ... load them up and fire them. Firing German artillery was like firing ours," Sanderson recalled. "We had a ram staff. They didn't. They'd just use their fist. Slam it in with your fist. Catch the hammer as it would be coming back. Sometimes smoke would be coming back as you opened them.

"I always thought me and my assistant driver, because we got that special detail—we were by ourselves with no backup. The First Army gave the captain a Bronze Star so he could hand [it] out to whoever he pleased in his outfit. Why give it to a prime mover driver? All he did was move the guns." Sanderson didn't think it was fair to be pulled out on detail, unprotected by his remaining troops. "That's where the Bronze Star should have gone. We had five battle stars. One more battle and we would have gotten a Bronze Star."

Sanderson got plenty of special detail. They took him and his assistant driver to a huge field at night so they could run a wire for their phones. "A jeep would drive the wire across the field. They'd say, 'Here, this is your position.' It was right next to a row of turnips. The Germans planted huge rows of them. A row of turnips covered in brush used to feed their animals and troops. We were out there to report if they [the German troops] came in by parachute. We were sitting ducks out there in the middle of the friggin' field. All by ourselves, you know. These kind of details, you don't mind when you're back with your men. But when you're all by yourself, those kinds of detail kind of get scary." Sanderson added, "They'd come by and drop those personnel bombs. They'd drop them all over the place and they'd go pop, pop, pop all over the friggin' place like popcorn. They also dropped flares so they could see. They'd see us sitting ducks next to the pile of turnips camouflaged like it was something else. I was probably nineteen years old."

Chapter 5

People Don't Know What
It Is to Be Scared

"When you can't see it, you get scared. You don't know where it's coming from. Anyone who said they weren't scared is a damn liar."

The war had been over for more than seventy years when Charlie and I spoke about his life. The memory of his war efforts is etched in his mind as though they had happened yesterday—just like the others I've interviewed, they all seem to remember the war in great details. There was lots of smoke, fire, guns going off, aircraft strafing; it was war, with people being killed on a regular basis.

In 1947, Sanderson went to work for a small company called P. J. Keating, a supplier of asphalt and ready-made concrete. There was just Sanderson and one other worker running the company's Lunenburg, Massachusetts, location. "I'd open up the doors in the morning and lock up at night," explained Sanderson. The equipment consisted of old navy surplus items that the two men could run on their own. They'd power up the plant and get it all running. Sanderson worked there for forty-two years, retiring in 1986. He was very good friends with the founders, both P. J. Keating and his son, Warren Keating. Today, the small company Sanderson helped build employs more than three hundred people.

Tech Corporal Charles M. Sanderson, thank you for sharing your stories with us, and thank you for your service keeping America safe during wartime.

SANDERSON AS A TRUCK DRIVER.

SANDERSON (LEFT) STOPPING FOR A PHOTO
SHOOT DURING ONE OF MANY MARCHES.

THE SEER BRIDGE.

BRIDGES THE SOLDIERS MADE FROM PONTOONS
TO CARRY TROOPS AND VEHICLES.

PRIME-MOVER TOWING A CANNON TOWARDS BATTLE.

SANDERSON'S TROOPS DURING INSPECTION.

TROOPS DURING A FULL INVASION WITH
PROTECTION OF AIR, SEA AND LAND.

SANDERSON'S "GUN" OF CHOICE.

MASSIVE HOWITZER CANNON.
NOTE THE SOLDIER BLOCKING HIS EARS FOR PROTECTION.

SIDE VIEW ALSO FROM SANDERSON'S PRIVATE COLLECTION.

Book 6

STAFF SERGEANT ALBERT GEORGE PINARD

Chapter 1

It Turned Out to Be a Terrible, Bloody War

Albert Pinard was born on April 26, 1925, in Worcester, Massachusetts. He was one of seven children in a family with five girls and two boys. Ten years separated the two boys, Albert being the elder male.

"You were fortunate," Pinard said. "It all starts out as a young person, as a great adventure, but it doesn't really turn out that way."

Pinard's father was a World War I veteran. He was from Maine, and his mother was from Boston. The beginning of his story is a bit unusual. Originally, his mother married his father's brother. They had a child together and moved to Maine. While there, she met her husband's brother. Whereas one brother lived for himself, the other was better suited to her family's needs. Eventually, Wilfred Pinard married Margaret McGlauphin, and they had a family of their own that included Albert.

Pinard attended Worcester Trade School in Worcester, Massachusetts, to study automobile mechanics. Unfortunately, there "weren't many cars at that time," Pinard said of the 1930s. He learned mostly how to charge batteries and clean spark plugs. Like many of his generation, he didn't have the luxury of graduating from high school. In 1941, at the age of sixteen and out of school, Albert Pinard was searching for work to help support the family. He found work making boots at H. H. Brown in Worcester.

As we know, the United States was on the verge of war. Europe was aflame, and the Japanese were invading China. "There was a lot of war," recalled Pinard about those days long ago. We were feeding Europe military supplies and food. That didn't sit well with Germany, having us supplying their enemies. Warnings were out that if the United States entered certain waters, we risked being destroyed—and many ships and supplies were destroyed, as history showed us. "It was only a matter of time before we were at war with either Japan or Germany," reported Pinard.

Like many of the kids growing up during the Depression era, Pinard heard plenty of stories from the old-timers about World War I. War was spoken of "as a glorious thing. They don't always mention the dead." Pinard recalled many stories from his dad about the war to end all wars, as everyone had hoped it would be, such as how they'd drunk wine and eaten exotic foods in France and danced with French women. But they never much talked about being in the trenches. That was the real war. "There wasn't much glory to it," Pinard said. "It was dirty, cold, and wet. And when they did have action, it was a slaughter. It was machine guns against human bodies trying to take the machine guns out. The only glamorous part of it was the air wars," he continued. "The types of planes they had engaged in dogfights." Even today, he seemed to have retained a sense of romanticism alongside the realities of war.

By now, the economy was starting to boom. The United States was feeding England and Russia on the Lend-Lease program, transferring supplies to them that they'd pay for or return later. The Depression was at an end, and the economy was thriving. "Worcester had a lot of machine shops and shoe and boot shops. We were making boots for Russian troops," Pinard explained.

Chapter 2

A Seventeen-Year-Old
United States Marine

P inard enlisted in the United States Marine Corps the day he turned seventeen, April 26, 1942.

By June 17, 1942, he was officially US government property. When he was sworn in and raised his right hand, he was asked, "Regular or reserve?"

He answered, "Regular. I want to be a marine." As a result, his hitch was four solid years, 1942 to 1946. "Reserve" would have meant to the end of the war plus six months, if the United States so chose. The marines were used primarily in the Pacific theater.

Like most East Coast marines, Pinard stopped first in Parris Island, South Carolina. In 1942, the United States instituted six weeks of rigorous basic marine training (eight weeks if you were in the San Diego, California, facility). Although called "basic," it was brutal training for combat, supervised by military leaders who had experienced actual combat. They would push men to their limits and back. It all started with indoctrination training, then moved on to six-plus hours of bayonet training; forty-five hours of close-order drill training; thirty-six hours of field training that included first aid, tenting, combat exercises, and patrolling; and at least seventy hours of rifle training. Every minute was accounted for and put to good use. Physical conditioning and extensive marching were not included in those hours. They were extra—until the men became as sharp as knives.

In November 1941, the last month of peacetime, more than 2,000 recruits joined the marines. December saw more than 10,000, and January 1942 had an incredible 22,600 enlistments. They were living in tents as a result of an enormous expansion of the barracks. War was upon us, and things were happening at a bullet's speed. At that time, the marines were expanding their air corps for ground support—meaning the gunnery aircraft could shoot down on the enemy, blow up bridges, destroy factories, and cause havoc while allowing the ground troops to move forward with air cover.

Military officials looked at Pinard's record and saw that he had experience as an auto mechanic, so they sent him for an additional five months of training as a machinist's mate at an army school in Jacksonville, Florida. Pinard then volunteered for aerial gunner school, followed by advanced aerial gunnery training in Hollywood, Florida. There, he would shoot at sleeves being towed by other aircraft to sharpen his shooting skills. He'd sit in a turret or other aircraft, firing round after round of ammo and skeet shooting to learn how to lead his shots. He was trained even further in strafe gunning, dive-bombing, radio communications, and radar reading.

Pinard was just about eighteen years old now and getting a world of experience and knowledge to last him his lifetime. And he hadn't met the enemy yet; he hadn't looked into their eyes, smelled the smoke from their bombs, or realized the doors he was about to enter.

Next up, he was heading to the West Coast and embarking on an ocean liner headed for New Caledonia, wherever that was.

"All marines are riflemen. No matter what you do, you're a rifleman. Always have the full pack, bayonet, helmet, M-1 rifle, gas mask," Pinard said. In Southern California, he recalled, there were long lines of marines getting on board the ocean liner; it seemed like miles and miles of soldiers, long hours of just waiting in full gear. Pinard stood at the end of the line. As a result, he didn't have a bunk or a place of his own. He was stuck sleeping on the main deck of the ship for sixteen days with very little shelter—in rain, shine, whatever. This was the fun part of being a marine during World War II.

Pinard served his country, fighting the Japanese in the Solomon Islands Campaign in the Pacific theater. "You gotta remember, this is the Pacific fighting with the Japanese. When I went overseas, it was still tenuous. We were still fighting in the Solomon Islands. That went on for a year, year and a half ... naval battle after naval battle. Continuous. It was fighting, fighting, fighting. That was a war unto itself, the Solomons. But that turned the tide of the war," he explained proudly.

After the difficult and bloody but successful Battle of the Midway Islands, the United States had gained some momentum and a morale boost. The Midway Islands had previously been the departure area for the Japanese to bomb Pearl Harbor. In June 1942, the Douglas SBD Dauntless dive-bomber aircraft sank four Japanese carriers, but that war was far from over or decisive. The United States invaded Guadalcanal before spending two years fighting in the Solomon Islands and the Bismarck Archipelago, knowing the biggest Japanese air base at the time was in Rabaul, in New Guinea. The Japanese had five airstrips and a harbor there, protected by plenty of surface-to-air arms—all targets of opportunity.[20]

Upon Pinard's arrival in the South Pacific, his first stop was the Russell Islands, where he was quickly assigned a subgroup. He was then sent to New Caledonia and on to Guadalcanal. There, he got his first taste of war. The Japanese were fighting for this small piece of land. It's the largest of the Solomon Islands, but still only two thousand square miles—a bit larger than the state of Connecticut, made of volcanic ash

---

20 https://www.ibiblio.org/hyperwar/USMC/USMC-M-CSol/USMC-M-CSol-1.html.

with a spiked peak over 7,500 feet. The interior is made up mostly of small rivers and dense wooded forests and lined with mangrove swamps and lots of hungry crocodiles. The shorelines are beautiful beaches, lined with coconut trees and beautiful vegetation that can flourish only in volcanic-rich soil—all to be plowed over, bombed, and destroyed from the battles of war.

Pinard was part of the new replacements who slept in tents up on a hilly area from which they watched the battles down below. He clearly remembers ships being torpedoed, sinking day and night. Every night there were air raids, with antiaircraft guns blazing and going off in all directions. The sounds of the big gun blasts and noise must have been incredible. "Guadalcanal was under heavy air fighting at that time," he said. "During the daytime, you'd see them dogfighting upstairs, antiaircraft shooting. And during the night, there was a lot of it going on."

A typical 90 mm antiaircraft gun weighed in at almost twenty thousand pounds, was more than ten feet tall, and could put a twenty-four-pound shell in the air at a rate of twenty-five per minute. Ringing ears and partial deafness seemed to follow many of the veterans home with their memories. "Anyone who had anything that had to do with artillery has to be deaf," added Pinard.

For a reference, the Solomon Islands are approximately 3,500 miles southwest of Hawaii and 3,500 miles southeast of Japan, but only 1,000 miles southwest off the coast of Australia—very far from Worcester, Massachusetts.

Chapter 3

Fighting Japanese from the Sky

Pinard was originally assigned as an engine mechanic's mate to replace Pratt & Whitney's eighteen-cylinder engines in the beautiful Vought F4U Corsair aircraft. The engines were shipped to them in huge wooden crates. Included in the crates were all the tools he would need for the job. The engines were completely covered in a Vaseline-type coating called cosmoline to prevent rust and salt water from entering the interior and cylinders of the engines. Pinard had the monotonous job of taking them apart, removing safety-wired nuts and bolts, and then inspecting the interior of the cylinders to make sure they were safe for flight. Only after the rigorous inspection was complete could Pinard switch them into another aircraft. This was his duty for his first five months in the Solomon Islands.

From Guadalcanal, Pinard went back to the Russell Islands to join a Marine Air Group—number 21, to be specific. On a side note about MAG-21, during the attack on Pearl Harbor on December 7, 1941, the group had seventeen casualties, and all twenty-one of their aircraft were destroyed. They were, however, put back together, fighting many of the major battles in the Pacific. Pinard was in the Russell Islands, assigned to the New Hebrides, just south of the Solomon Islands and north of New Caledonia. He ended up spending more than five months on New Hebrides. While there, Pinard went to a gunners pool and was assigned to the VMSB 235, then the VMSB 236 to fly combat missions in the Douglas SBD Dive Bombers.[21]

The Douglas SBD was a dive-bomber made for the navy and marines during the war. It was an amazing aircraft that Pinard found himself strapped into as an aerial gunner. The 1,000-plus-horsepower aircraft proved to be very effective. Between 1940 and 1944, the United States built 24,000 of them—an amazing logistical feat by itself. These aircraft found their targets and enemy fighters with ease and grace. They had two seats, for a pilot and a gunner, sitting back to back. The pilot manned his own fixed mounted guns and was the bombardier. The rear-facing gunner protected the ship after the pilot released its bombs on a target and flew for safer grounds. They shot nonstop, and the Japanese shot back. The pilot had two large .50-caliber mounted guns, and the rear gunner had two .30-caliber mounted guns. The aircraft also carried an additional 2,250 pounds of bombs. It could travel more than 1,200 miles at more than 250 mph at altitudes over 25,000 feet, if needed.

As dive-bombers, they dove vertically straight down at the target, employing perforated dual flaps as speed brakes to not overstress the airframe from flying out of control or breaking apart. They then dropped their bombs at very low altitudes directly at the target, maximizing their accuracy by aiming the nose of the aircraft where they wanted to drop their bombs. After releasing the bombs and then leveling off the aircraft, usually as low as two hundred feet—which causes great stress on both the aircraft and pilot and gunner—they rapidly pulled the aircraft back up, creating even more stress and g-factors. Knowing and controlling the g-factor, the pilot literally grunted the blood back into his head and brain while the gunner just kept shooting, knowing and waiting for the g's to take control of his body—even into a short

---

21 https://en.m.wikipedia.org/wiki/Marine_Aviation_Training_Support_Group_21 https://en.m.wikipedia.org/wiki/VMF-236.

blackout stage. The aircraft then headed out and over the open sea, but still wasn't fully out of harm's way.

During these raids, their rapidly changing altitudes meant the pilot and gunner were exposed to every kind of antiaircraft weaponry. Pinard explained what some of his battles in this aircraft were like. "Flying above ten thousand feet, we were supposed to use oxygen. The missions were that you took off over the water, of course, flew at about five or six thousand feet until we were over the target, then climb to fifteen thousand feet. We were up there for only about fifteen or twenty minutes. We didn't have oxygen on our plane. We flipped the plane over on its back and dove straight down from fifteen thousand feet. The dive brakes would open and our speed would be limited to about 250 miles per hour. Otherwise, you'd be out of control ... carrying three bombs, a thousand-pounder under the fuselage and a couple more hundred-pounders under each wing. We went after our target, dropped our bombs at about two thousand feet, aiming straight down. By the time you pulled out, you were at 250 feet above the ground, heading towards the ocean to get the hell away from their guns.

"There would be about twenty planes to a squadron," Pinard continued. "We'd fly a loose formation after being engaged by antiaircraft guns on the ground ... each made to destroy one another. We had three layers of protection in the air. At thirty thousand feet, the P-38s were watching over us. Aside of us were usually the big fighter Corsairs. Below us were New Zealanders, flying their P-40s under five thousand feet. They'd be strafing too and staying with us.

"The pilot would be strafing on the way down, and then I'd be strafing on the way out. Once you get over the g's, you have your hands on the guns. Then, all of a sudden, the pilot starts to pull up. You can't hold on to the guns anymore, so your hands go on your lap—if you're leaning forward at all—your head and body lean forward between your legs. There's nothing you can do about it. Things then start to get all hazy as hell. Sometimes you actually black out, but you come right back. Then it lessens up and you start thinking about those damn antiaircraft guns. We'd be between mountains sometimes, and they'd be shooting down on us from both sides and at us [laterally] from the sides and up from the ground.

"As quickly as you could, you'd undo your seat belt, stand up in the plane, and turn the turret guns and hold the triggers down two thousand rounds and watch your tracers. The way the guns were loaded, every five rounds you had two copper rounds, a steel armor piercing, an incendiary, and a tracer. You just strafed the living hell out of it. Sometimes the pilot would be yelling, 'The other side, the other side,' so you'd just swivel that thing around and hold down the triggers." The noise level, shaking of the aircraft, shots being fired back at them, and need for more speed to get away even faster had to have been terrifying.

Tracers are bullets with small amounts of pyrotechnic charges in them. When ignited, the shooters can see their aim better. But at night, they light up the sky and the target. The shooter can aim and shoot without spending time on the sights or finding the target.

Pinard's crew flew with the cockpit canopy back, open-cockpit-style, near the equator. At sea level, it was very hot. At about six thousand feet, it was comfortable. But at fifteen thousand feet, they were freezing and shaking from the sweat that exuded from them at lower altitudes—a difference of almost seventy degrees Fahrenheit between altitudes. They had made many of those flights, mostly with the same pilot. His airman logbook shows *STRIKES*. Pinard received 50 percent extra pay for flying those, but it sure wasn't all about the money. It was their job, their duty, and about our freedom to follow.

"Battle of Solomon Islands is a war unto itself. It went on for years," said Pinard. "The Solomon Islands had some of the war's most incredible battles. The Japanese were a very formidable and well-trained navy. We were trying to destroy their shipyards and landing strips. Almost everything had to be done from ships," continued Pinard. "We were surrounded by miles of open treacherous waters and smaller volcanic islands. The Japanese had been planning these invasions for years. They had tunnels throughout the mountainous terrain that were well hidden. There was very little easily spotted from the air."

Chapter 4

Targets of Opportunity

Pinard flew from Rabaul to New Ireland, a short fifty- to hundred-mile hop, to search for opportunities. "We'd go after bridges a lot," Pinard said. "Everyone would separate. I'd spot a small jungle bridge, and we'd go after it. The Japanese always had plenty more of guns and tracers shooting at us. I'd call my pilot on the radio and say, 'You know, we're getting a lot of tracers back here.' He'd say, 'Don't be jealous. I'm getting a lot up here too!' Hitting a small bridge while being shot at is difficult. He [the pilot] dropped the big bomb right away. We often missed the target, and it landed in the water. We went back down after it two more times and dropped one bomb each time, the pilot strafing all the way down and I'm strafing all the way back up.

"The trick is to put the plane right down on the deck. When a plane is coming at you that fast, a couple hundred feet off the ground, it's hard for them to get their aim. Once we were finally over the ocean, the only thing we had to worry about was big shore guns that the Japanese had. They were usually used for shooting at warships, but they'd shoot those big guns at us too. They'd try to get us with the waterspouts from the bombs going into the water. The spouts from the blasts could get at high as five hundred feet, and we were well below that.

"Sometimes we'd be part of a real big raid, big for the South Pacific. We had P-38s Corsairs, P-40s, Grumman TBM Avengers, and us. The

TBM glided in to drop their bombs. We came in right behind them straight down from fifteen thousand feet to act as additional firepower for them to drop their bombs, working together. We flew a lot of missions with the same guys. Even our tents were close by. Many were New Zealanders—damn nice guys and great pilots."

Pinard flew combat missions for four straight months before shuttling off for some much-needed R&R to Sydney, Australia, for a week. Then he went back and did it all over again.

After Pinard spent fifteen months in the South Pacific as a combat flying marine, the government sent him home to the States. The men were considered to have served their duty and were homeward bound— but not for long. Pinard was home for only a couple of months, enjoying the smells of home-cooked food and American soil, when he was sent back over toward the end of 1944. The United States still needed more troops. Being unmarried and with no family to support, Pinard was ordered to fulfill his four-year promise, and back over to the South Pacific he went for another five-month tour.

Once again, Pinard was flying the dangerous skies in various aircraft, doing his job, unwaveringly, to defeat the Japanese Imperial Army. From Guam to Tinian into Iwo Jima and finally to Okinawa, he prepared and fought for what they were all hoping would be the final invasion of Japan—knowing it would be bloody hell and that the Japanese would fight till their last soldier's final breath.

On Pinard's second trip, he flew in medium bombers, twin-engine Mitchell B-25s, renamed as PBJs. Pinard was reassigned to the VMB-612 squadron; their job was to hinder and harass the Japanese day and night. (*VMB* stood for *volar*, or "fly" in French; "marine"; and "bombing.") They flew in every type of weather thrown at them—they were, after all, marines. Whether in heavy rain, gusting winds, thick ominous clouds, or against talented war-hardened Japanese Zero fighter planes, the boys were out doing their jobs. His crew was under the command of Lieutenant Colonel Jack R. Cram, also known as Mad Jack, and his squadron was nicknamed Cram's Ram. In all and by the war's end, seven squadrons of PBJs saw combat in the Pacific. It was a tough crew pitted against a tough adversary. They suffered the loss of forty-five aircraft—twenty-six in combat and nineteen in noncombat operations—and 173 precious lives—111 enlisted men and 62 officers.

The previous couple of months before Pinard joined the VMB-612, things were terrible. Although they managed to destroy a submarine, four medium-sized freighters, and one large freighter in a couple of days, November cost them two aircraft and thirteen men. The troops were devastated by the losses. These were small groups of marines, five or six soldiers per aircraft. When Pinard joined up with them during the Saipan phase in 1945, the VMB-612 flew 335 missions and counted forty-nine attacks on ships. By April 1945, Pinard and the VMB-612 were in Iwo Jima, finally within striking distance of southern Japan. But the month of April would prove to be heartbreaking again.

April saw the loss of four aircraft and crews through three operational accidents and the downing of another PBJ by two friendly fighters. There was very little to show for their actions, except for the loss of those four aircraft and the deaths of six men. It was a bitter pill to swallow; Cram's squadron suffered further losses as it searched for enemy shipping near the Bonin Islands.

VMB-612 was stationed on Iwo Jima from April 10 to July 28. It flew 251 sorties, with eighty-three of those targets located and fifty-three vessels damaged or sunk. On July 13, echelons of VMB-612 began arriving on Okinawa and were placed under the operational control of Fleet Air Wing 1. They began antishipping sweeps along the northwestern coast of Kyushu.

Even during the closing days of the war and with very few targets, Cram's Rams made an impressive show for themselves. Between August

1 and 15, the Rams flew thirty-one sorties, damaging approximately twenty enemy vessels.

In the Central Pacific, VMB-613 turned over its PBJs for disposal in October and was decommissioned on November 21, leaving Pinard's VMB-612 as the last PBJ squadron in the Pacific. On November 8, 1945, VMB-612 left for the United States, where it was decommissioned on March 14, 1946, officially ending the US Marine Corps' use of the PBJ Mitchell.[22]

Pinard explained that the PBJs were narrow and that shooting from both sides meant that the gunner had to run back and forth, from side to side. There were also turret gunners. Mad Jack had taken the two bomb doors off the PBJ and hung two rockets on them. They were about twelve feet long and were called Tiny Tims. They flew at night to find the ships, fire the rockets, and have a photographer there to photograph the hits using the rockets as the light for their cameras. Flying at night in the South Pacific had to be incredibly disorienting— add to that the flying maneuvers to drop the rockets, banking the plane over for the cameraman, and returning to base, all without being shot down, getting lost, or hitting another aircraft, while still keeping the ship upright and steady.

"There was a crew and myself, and we had one tent. We were waiting there while the rest of the guys went out on a mission. They never came back. I was alone in that damn tent for about two days," Pinard remembered sadly. "Eventually, I was one of the last marines to leave Iwo Jima and head to Okinawa."

In Rabaul, there were high volcanic peaks and low valley areas. Large winding, flowing rivers flowed between the peaks below, leading into a big harbor. The Japanese shipping was suffering from the army, navy, and marines' constant barrage. "They were now using small boats

---

22 https://www.mca-marines.org/leatherneck/marine-corps-b-25-squadrons-world-war-ii#.dpuf Alan C. Carey.

to ship their supplies," Pinard said. "They'd use these barges at night to supply all their different bases; they came out of Rabaul. These barges were thirty to forty feet long, made of steel, and armed to the teeth. There were many epic battles between them and our navy PT boats. They'd hide them during the day, camouflage them. But they were in the river, hundreds and hundreds of them," he recalled.

"We wanted to kill their supply lines, so we went after those barges. Our mission was to come inland, come in between the mountains, strafe, and drop our bombs on those barges ... Then it was off to sea. They had guns everywhere, shooting down at us, across at us, and up at us. To me, the most dangerous thing was, you'd have them shooting 90 mms, exploding shells, tracers, and all that, and they're dangerous but better for high altitudes. As a dive-bomber, we'd have these Swedish design guns called Bofors with four barrels, a big round of ammo with clips of 40 mm. But when you came down on the deck, they'd be firing everything at us. They had 20s, 30s, 40s small arms, all shooting at us as we were going out between the peaks. At this mission there were army fighters, P-38s medium bombers ... all kinds of flights, one of the bigger fights. A few hundred planes all going at this. But it was not very coordinated. They were all separate and going at the same time at the targets.

"The exciting thing on this was we knew we were going to be getting a lot of fire. We knew the gunners had to be ready, recover from the g's, stand up, get over the side. A lot of times you're shooting up 'cause they're shooting down and there are tracers everywhere.

"Typically, when you're on a mission, you have what they call radio silence. You don't talk to each other over the radio because it helps the enemy radio-detection finders find you. They can home in on the radio waves and locate your position. You can talk to one another in your plane, but not to other planes—unless it's a real emergency. When that was under way, the Japanese must have had a field day. You knew when a plane was going down because they were calling out 'Mayday' or another plane would be calling it out for them and where the approximate place the plane was going down.

"On that mission, I was firing the damn thing over the side and I had trouble with my ring at that time," Pinard said feverishly, as if it had just occurred. "It wouldn't lock into position, and every time I fired, the recoil would pull to the other side, and I thought I was going to shoot my tail. But I had to muscle it over the side. The pilot is yelling, 'Over the other side ... over the other side.' I couldn't see them. I was so busy myself and, at the same time, they had all these calls for Mayday, Mayday, Mayday, Mayday. I'm thinking, *This many planes going down?* I couldn't see them myself. I was so busy myself."

Explaining how to stand up to shoot from a moving plane at an enemy shooting back, Pinard said, "You could stand up only so many times. We had to wear a helmet and goggles, and we had to have earphones. There was a push-to-talk handy. I could shoot and talk. I was nineteen when I was flying those combats. There was so much going on at one time. When you stand up—and I'm kind of tall, I could only stand up so much. You had to undo your safety harness because that's what holds you down. The front of the canopy protects you somewhat from the wind. I tried standing taller a couple of times, but you're going over two hundred miles per hour, and the wind takes your goggles and helmet and turns them sideways." It's not what you want as distraction added to the already mass confusion of being shot at— shooting to preserve your plane, the pilot, and your mission. Although the crew had had lots of training, that's not the same as real combat.

The planes were quickly getting worn from all the use and abuse. The seats were designed for seat-chutes made for that plane. But the men wore parachutes, measured to fit them. They had a four-point clip harness, and the seat hung down. When they sat in the plane, the seat cushion was part of the chute.

Pinard flew twenty-two of these missions. His outfit went through the entire Philippines. However, his stint was split into two, and he didn't travel the entire distance. His average mission was short, about two and a half hours by the time he got back.

"When I was on Iwo Jima, we had two airstrips," Pinard recalled. "We were flying off one, and the fighters were flying off the other. The fighters flying off the other strip were army P-51s, the most beautiful plane I'd ever seen in my life—brilliant silver. We needed Iwo Jima because of the distance of flying between Tinian and Saipan. We lost a lot of planes making the distance. All morning long, you'd hear one long loud roar of the B-29s on their way to Japan. Never in formation, they'd be all over the place, all over the damn sky at maybe twenty-five, thirty thousand feet. Late afternoon, they'd be on their way back. And that's when things got exciting. The only planes that were supposed to land on Iwo Jima were the 29s when they had a problem. After a raid, you'd see one great big long line of planes circling overhead, trying to come in. One would come in with an engine out, and another plane, not even in the circle, would cut him off. He had two engines out. The first guy would hit full throttles for all the power he had to go around again. They didn't know where to put all the planes. They just kept coming in where they'd pull off to the side of the strip and park."

The B-29 was called the Superfortress, and for good reason. She was 99 feet long with a wingspan of 141 feet, and 27 feet tall. It was a monster of an aircraft, weighing twenty thousand pounds, carrying ten thousand pounds of bombs. The crew of eleven could fly over thirty thousand feet at more than 350 mph with a range of more than 3,200 miles—faster and higher than any Japanese fighter plane. Upon landing, the ambulances drove back and forth between planes, saving the crews.

They had some relaxing time too. "The beaches were all black sand, all volcanic. There were ships sunk everywhere. We'd go swimming when we could, jump off the half-sunk ships with their masts sticking out of the water."

One time, Pinard saw a B-17 on Iwo Jima, an oddity, because those were used mainly in the European theater and hardly ever in the Pacific. Pinard approached the aircraft and noticed there was something attached under the belly where the bomb doors were. When he asked about it, he was told it was a boat with a parachute. Fighting in the South Pacific often meant flying over water for long periods of time until you reached your targets. The B-29 bombers and P-51 Mustang fighters that escorted them would return by passing over another island called Chichi Jima, about 150 miles north of Iwo Jima. When returning, the Mustangs would descend on Chichi Jima and strafe them as much as possible. Of course, the heavily armed Japanese would shoot some of them down. The B-17 would try to locate the pilots at sea and drop them a raft for safety and recovery. Pinard was talking to the crew when a call came in that another P-51 Mustang was down. Later that day, the same B-17 was back—only without its boat beneath the belly. When Pinard asked about the mission, he was told they had found the pilot and deployed the boat to him. The pilot couldn't get the motor to start on the boat and was getting closer and closer to the island. The Japanese were now dropping mortar bombs at the lone soldier. The B-17 crew said one finally managed to hit the boat and the pilot was killed. The crew didn't despair, but prepared to depart again soon—ideally to save another American life from being bombed, drowned, or becoming a Japanese POW on Chichi Jima.

For Pinard, if his plane or one similar went down in the water, they'd send a Catalina PBY (Patrolled Bomber—the Y was the code for the manufacturer) to the rescue. A PBY was a lumbering multiengine amphibious aircraft that would land in the open sea, mostly for search-and-rescue missions. Pinard had many friends picked up by the PBYs.

One of the pilots told Pinard how they had had a problem switching fuel tanks and had to ditch a tank in the water. The switch sending fuel to the engine got stuck; they had plenty of fuel in the other tank but couldn't get to it. They tried pushing and manhandling the switch, but to no avail. Eventually, knowing the inevitability of fuel starvation was coming quickly, they threw all their guns and ammo off the plane and ditch-landed it in the ocean. "The pilot has a small one-man raft attached to his chute; the gunner doesn't have one. Guess we know the soldier they valued the most," said Pinard, smiling. "On the side of the plane is a round trapdoor. In there is a round two-man rubber raft in a rubberized container with a compressed air container to inflate it. Before you make your water landing, you take all your chute harnesses off. You land, [and] the pilot jumps out on the wing and grabs onto the back of your belt. You lean all the way out, pull the trapdoor, pull the raft out, then pull the cord and it inflates. This is after it's in the water. The plane can stay up for about five minutes before sinking." It was important to make sure the pilot was conscious after landing. Otherwise, the crew had to pull him out first. Pinard never mentioned being shot at or bombed while this was happening—never mind the sharks in the warm South Pacific.

Another time, Pinard's fellow marines had ditched their plane in the water. They got the two-man raft out as they'd practiced many times. They jumped in and waited for the PBY to come get them. All of a sudden, they felt a bump ... and another bump. It was a shark. It was circling them, bumping the raft. Every time it bumped the raft, they'd hear a loud scraping noise. Sharks have rough hides, and the crew was afraid it would rip the raft. They always carried a .45 sidearm on their missions, so the pilot prepared to shoot the shark. The gunner said to him, "I don't know if we should shoot the shark. They'll be blood all over and those babies are gonna come from everywhere." They had a small paddle, and every time the shark came by, they hit it in the nose, hoping it would go away. They also had a small dye packet as part of their life vest. Once the dye was placed in the water, it would spread over twenty-five feet for up to three and a half hours, making search-and-rescue missions more successful. It helped when flying over large bodies of water, looking for a small life raft. The dye also included actual shark repellant, and it must have worked, because the shark left them alone.

Chapter 5

★

Morale Was Way Down— Then Came the Bomb

The army in Europe, with its B-17s, lost many planes, and there were many casualties. They had trouble sending those guys out for further missions. They didn't have good fighter protection until the P-51 Mustangs came along. "We were losing many pilots and soldiers, and morale was way down," Pinard said. "So what they started to do was make every aerial gunner in the air force, marines, and navy a staff sergeant. It didn't mean you had any more command. It just meant you'd get more money. That was the idea.

"I was on Okinawa when the atomic bomb went off. We'd never heard of an atomic bomb. I remember I was down on the air base, listening to the radio. They went to an American broadcast from the armed services to offset Tokyo Rose. They were talking about a bomb they'd dropped on Japan that had the strength of ten thousand pounds of TNT. So what? They continued to say the US had a couple more and were going to drop them if Japan didn't surrender. Now we were excited. We were getting ready to invade Japan, and none of us really wanted to. That would have been bloody.

"After the Nagasaki bomb was dropped, the Japanese surrendered a couple days later. I was on Okinawa and there was mostly Japanese. I had some work details after the surrender. I'd find one that could speak some English. I met one that was a schoolteacher before the war. We kept them busy cleaning up."

Pinard returned home and left the military as a staff sergeant. He gave his flying silk chit that he flew with to family members. The chit showed the water currents and area he was flying in, if they had to make an emergency water landing. His family has cherished it, even putting it in a two-way glass frame showing both sides. He served our country faithfully from his enlistment on June 17, 1942, until he received his honorable discharge on June 16, 1946. Staff Sergeant Albert G. Pinard received many medals and awards for his service to our country: the WWII Victory Medal, the Asiatic-Pacific Campaign Medal with three stars, the Good Conduct ribbon, Wings with three stars (for battle against an armed vessel, land based and enemy fighter), and a ribbon for serving in an American Possession (Guam).

Pinard said that many years later, when he got together with other veterans, they'd always remember the good times. "The drinking, the flying that made it [war] all glamorous as hell," Pinard said. "It was easy to get all wrapped up in it … easy to convince young men to fight for their country and the glorious days ahead. By the time they're in their forties, most men are smarter and in not such a hurry to get in harm's way as we were in our twenties."

An incredible historian, Pinard understands the leaderships of many countries from hundreds of years ago to the present, and how war would insidiously manifest itself out of greed and prejudice before it could be stopped. He understood how, for centuries, the Japanese thrived wonderfully and kept to themselves in their own country; how the German people felt shame about the end of World War I; why the American government passed discriminatory laws against Japanese Americans; and how Hitler would blame the Jews and other non-Aryans for the financial and social problems the Germans were enduring.

Pinard thinks that Pearl Harbor was everyone's fault and that we, as a country, knew it was coming at the time. "How could we expect a country to declare war and then lose the element of surprise?" he asked. "In the history of Japan, they've never declared war; they build up their offenses and go. Mainstream media helped encourage our entire country's full participation with songs, film clips, and 'extra' newspaper coverage. Wars make history. Without wars, there'd be no history."

Upon returning home after his duty, Pinard adjusted with some of the benefits of the new GI Bill. He called it a "wonderful thing for all the guys that lost a lot of time." Coming back unemployed, the returning soldiers were offered the "52-20 Club." They were entitled to twenty dollars per week for fifty-two weeks to give them time to readjust to civilian life, experience some normalcy, and find suitable work. Pinard lasted only a month unemployed and like many other veterans, decided to find work instead of collecting money for not working. The Boston and Albany Railroad had been greatly deteriorating during the war. He got a job replacing rails and ties. It turned out that other workers were veterans too. The group worked hard all day long. Pinard was employed there for a couple of years. During the winter, the job was tough, shoveling snow off the tracks to repair them. They all grew accustomed to difficult work, but at least no one was shooting at them.

Pinard held various other jobs after the railroad stint. TVs and their antennas started to appear everywhere in the early 1950s, and Pinard was part of the new revolution in television and home appliances. The early 1950s found him working at Gauthier's Appliance store in Worcester, Massachusetts. It was there that he met Kathleen "Bernice" Briggs. They were married in 1952. Together, they had a son, Edwin, and a daughter, Sharon. As of this writing, their family has grown to six grandchildren and eleven great-grandchildren. All these families were born and grew up thanks to Pinard's ability to survive such a nasty and brutal war.

Pinard eventually worked as a repairman of appliances and refrigeration equipment, retiring from Baypath in 1993. In the 1970s, Pinard finally obtained his own private pilot's certificate, flying small general aviation aircraft around friendly skies without a worry. He even took his wife up for a ride in the Piper Cub that he was fond of.

Today, at over ninety years of age, Albert Pinard still works with the Oxford Honor Guard providing US military funerals during veterans' funeral services.

Staff Sergeant Albert G. Pinard, thank you for your service and sacrifice to this great country.

PINARD'S CREW.

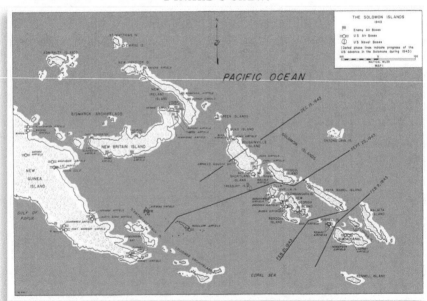

PINARD WOULD SEARCH FOR "TARGETS OF
OPPORTUNITIES" THROUGHOUT THESE ISLANDS.

DOUGLAS SBD DAUNTLESS DIVE BOMBER, SIMILAR TO PINARD AS A BACK SEAT GUNNER.

LOG BOOK ENTRY FOR PINARD'S 29 MISSIONS, JULY 1944. NOTE "STRIKE."

HORRORS OF WAR FROM PINARD'S
COLLECTION OF PRIVATE PHOTOS.

MASS OPEN GRAVES.

HUMAN BURNED REMAINS AS SOLDIERS LOOK ON IN DISBELIEF.

THE SOLOMON ISLANDS WHERE PINARD WOULD REGULARLY
PATROL BETWEEN GUADALCANAL AND NEW BRITAIN ISLANDS.

SBD DAUNTLESS ON PATROLS.

Book 7

STAFF SERGEANT
SANTO J. DiSALVO

Chapter 1

Tough Families in Tough Times

S anto DiSalvo and I met on several occasions to discuss his life. His family and mine were close friends, as were most of the old Sicilian families in our community. Everyone was called "cuz," because they all half believed they were actually cousins. He taught me a lot about my own family history that otherwise would have died off with the old-timers. He knew my father's brother Giuseppe, "Joe," who was killed during the war. He remembered coming home from the war and Joe not being around anymore. No one said anything to him, and he didn't ask. This lack of discussion and the acceptance of death was one example of how their lives had been drastically altered by the end of World War II. DiSalvo was ninety-three years young when we met, his mind as sharp as his glare as he remembered more nightmarish details than he was willing to share. He said right up front, "I haven't spoken to anybody about the war. I'm not going into any horror stories. I could, but I'm not going to."

Santo was born at the family home on Third Street in Fitchburg, Massachusetts, on November 5, 1922. His parents, Lucio and Vincenza, were from the province of Messina, in Sicily, and came to America sometime before 1910, part of a large group of Sicilians who immigrated to Fitchburg between 1900 and 1920. Work was plentiful, and they studied to become American citizens. DiSalvo's father was a bricklayer, and his mom stayed home to manage the nest.

The DiSalvos had seven children, including Santo. The first two—a boy and a girl—passed away at three and five years old, before the others were born. In the days before modern medicine, such casualties were, unfortunately, somewhat common. Of the five children who followed, there were three girls, Josephine, Catherine, and Rose, and two boys, Santo and his brother, Antonino. Antonino and one of his sisters were named after the deceased children, a common practice in those times.

The boys were both soldiers during World War II. Antonino "Tony" was two years older than Santo and was already married when war broke out. "I didn't even know he was in the war. When I went in, they weren't drafting married men. I didn't find out he was there until I came home," DiSalvo said, still in disbelief.

In 1939, at seventeen years old, DiSalvo found various jobs, from working in insect control to tearing down old barracks with nothing more than a basic nail puller to building roads in the small Massachusetts town of Athol. Most of the world was at war, and the United States was waiting for its call. And that call came on a Sunday morning, December 7, 1941, when Japan attacked Hawaii. The citizens of the United States were furious and ready to fight.

Chapter 2

My Number Came Up

On March 5, 1943, fifteen months after Pearl Harbor was attacked, Santo J. DiSalvo was drafted into the United States Army at the young age of twenty. The next 790 days of his life would change him forever.

DiSalvo reported to Fort Devens, Massachusetts, for initial sign-in and then went home for a week to get ready for war. He was ordered back to Fort Devens on March 12 to get formally sworn in, then issued his uniform and trucked off to Spartanburg, South Carolina, for basic military training. From there he went to another camp in New York before being quickly sent overseas to Oran, in Algeria. He was shipped there on the *Queen Mary* along with many other new soldiers heading to war, because replacements were urgently needed. It took them ten long days to reach North Africa.

A common theme with respect to World War II soldiers has been the strong bond between the men in combat. This real perception would be reinforced by the media, with the scores of World War II movies over the decades and the popularity of the two television miniseries *Band of Brothers* and *The Pacific*. Although the image of brotherhood is accurate, the replacement policy implemented by the army during World War II was detrimental to unit cohesion. The reality was that the bonds of brotherhood between new soldier replacements who hadn't seen real action and those who had been fighting and were battle hardened were often tested.

Replacing soldiers killed and wounded in combat units during the war was done on an individual basis. In World War II, except for those soldiers who arrived as a unit at the beginning of the war, men were sent individually to units to replace casualties. Rather than pulling battle-depleted units off the line and replacing them in combat with fresh, rested units, Army Chief of Staff George Marshall and General Leslie McNair, commander of Army Ground Forces, implemented the individual replacement system. Unlike the German military, which replaced entire decimated units with similarly trained units, the Americans deemed it logistically difficult to transport across oceans the equipment necessary to arm an entire replacement unit. Instead, the American Army strategy was to create replacement depots, called "repple-depples" or "repo-depos" by the GIs. These depots were near the battlefronts, so that generals could send individual soldiers to companies and battalions to replace the men lost. Even early in the war, the number of replacements was high. For example, in *The Deadly Brotherhood: The American Combat Soldier in World War II*,[23] John McManus notes that in Italy, in 1943, "only 34 percent of the infantrymen in line companies came overseas with their units" (p. 308), a fact that illustrates the heavy number of casualties by that point in the war.[24]

Private Santo J. DiSalvo was in Company G, 143rd Infantry Regiment, Thirty-Sixth Division. Infantry soldiers carried at least an M1 carbine rifle, three hand grenades, and plenty of ammunition. Officers had sidearms as well; the handgun was the standard-issue Model 1911 .45-caliber. About 1.9 million of those handguns were

---

23 "The deadly brotherhood: The American combat soldier in WWII." John C. McManus. Published Novato CA. Presidio c1998.

24 http://www.defensemedianetwork.com/stories/the-u-s-world-war-ii-troop -replacement-policy/.

made during World War II. Soon DiSalvo would be using a Thompson submachine gun that was almost as tall as he was. "It could fire fifteen shots," DiSalvo said of the Thompson. "The Germans were scared of that because they knew it went in small and came out big. It was a .45 [caliber]. The thing weighed eleven pounds."[25]

In the next couple of years, DiSalvo traveled from his quiet hometown of Fitchburg to Africa, Italy, France, Germany, and finally Austria with a bunch of men carrying guns and weapons, fighting a very clever and well-prepared German-led army. The entire time, he was mostly on foot, walking his way through the hills and countryside with his fellow troops, with occasional rides in trucks or on top of tanks.

---

25   http://www.militaryfactory.com/smallarms/ww2-us-infantry-regiment-guns.asp.

Chapter 3

Malaria

Operation Torch was designed for American troops to invade Salerno, Italy (thirty-five miles south of Naples) from Oran, in North Africa. Sicily had already been liberated from the German Third Reich and was now occupied by American and British forces. In 1943, a massive push to the Italian mainland was planned. The US Fifth Army led by the commanding general, Lieutenant General Mark W. Clark, and his Thirty-Sixth, Thirty-Fourth, Forty-Fifth, and Third Divisions along with the British X Corps had a definitive plan for the invasion. Based on intelligence showing the Italian soldiers and its civilians were tired of the war, an Allied invasion of this magnitude would only prove to be successful. The fact that Italian dictator and Nazi supporter Benito Mussolini had been removed from power July 25, 1943, helped the Allied cause as well as the Italians.

DiSalvo was included in the replacements for that invasion. Coincidentally, there were twelve men from Fitchburg in the same barracks and companies. "By September 1943, most of the Italians didn't want to fight; their own relatives were in America," DiSalvo remembered. It must have been tough for the Italian and American soldiers, worrying about fighting their own family members who had immigrated to the United States just a few years before the war.

"The Italians didn't want that war," DiSalvo said. "They often surrendered, and brutally killed Mussolini when the war was over." He remembered a story from Ralph Christofono, one of his hometown friends who was stationed in Sicily. "One time, he had a whole regiment of Italians surrender to him. The Italians were allies of the Germans, but were sent to the fronts to be killed while the Germans stayed back in the woods." This didn't sit well with other Italian troops.

The trip from Oran, Algeria, to Salerno, Italy, was a D-day of its own, a diversion from France as well as to invade Hitler's "Fortress Europe." Before this much-needed invasion, the Allies had annihilated the Nazi troops in Tunisia in May 1943, followed by the important island of Sicily in August after a bloody thirty-eight-day battle.[26]

In September 1943, the United States Fifth Army's Third Division—with Santo DiSalvo—was ready. After months of practice dry runs in North Africa, the daring plan was about to be carried out. D-day started with four divisions of both American and British troops, followed up with another eight divisions on a second wave. Commanding General Clark chose September 9 as D-day; the hour was set for 0330. Like the D-day invasion of Normandy that followed on June 6, 1944, this one was to be carried out in LCMs (landing craft, mechanized) and LCVPs (landing craft, vehicle, personnel), carrying troops and vehicles across treacherous waters toward a prepared and waiting foe.

At one minute past midnight on 9 September, loudspeakers on the transports called the first boat teams to their stations. Soldiers clambered down the nets into landing craft. Motors sputtered and then roared as the first boats pulled away. Soon the calm sea was alive with snub-nosed craft, circling to reach their proper positions. In the darkness some of the coxswains

26 http://www.history.army.mil/books/wwii/salerno/sal-prep.htm.

failed to locate their leaders. Lanes had been previously swept through the mine fields, but occasionally mines broke free and drifted into the paths which the boats were trying to follow. Spray drenched the men and their equipment. Many of the soldiers became seasick. But at length the LCM's and LCVP's carrying the first assault waves, turned east behind the guide boats toward the rendezvous deployment line, 6,000 yards from the Salerno beaches.[27]

DiSalvo must have contracted malaria while in Africa. He was on Italian soil for only two days when he started suffering from symptoms. Malaria has flu-like symptoms that come in cycles. DiSalvo was sent to an aid station; there were no hospitals in the field of battle. The malaria took its toll on him for almost three grueling weeks, with chills, fevers, sweats, nausea, and vomiting. Once healthy, DiSalvo rejoined his outfit, which was outside of Naples, heading to the Battle of San Pietro.

The Battle of San Pietro, fought December 8–17, 1943, was brutal and considered a major battle. The Germans had the area fortified on high points known as the Winter Line—in particular Mount Sambucaro and Mount Lungo. DiSalvo remembered there was a big monastery on a hill, a high lookout for the Germans. However, in order to move north to liberate Rome, they'd have to take San Pietro. The battles were raging fiercely at this point.

"We lost a lot of men, a lot of men," DiSalvo recalled sadly. "The Germans had what they called an eighty-eight, a big mortar. They were shelling us like it was raining. I was behind a wall when we were

---

27 www.history.army.mil/books/wwii/salerno/sal-fm.htm 10-09-2016.

in San Pietro. There was a big monastery up on a hill. The Germans could see us, and everyone that tried to take that hill took a beating. We didn't want to bomb the monastery. But they had to. There was no way to cross the river."

Interestingly enough, this also may have marked the first time Italian troops, First Italian Motorized Group, fought alongside Allied troops against the German Army. The battle is well documented, explaining further attacks and counterattacks. This was part of a bigger picture to breach the Bernhardt/Reinhard Line, which was six miles deep. It took a total of six weeks of heavy fighting to destroy those German defenses. The Fifth Army suffered sixteen thousand casualties from early November through late December 1943, along with massive damage to both towns and civilians. John Huston's film *The Battle of San Pietro* shows the accounts of those brutal weeks of war.

DiSalvo spent much of the war moving on the front lines. During this time, most of his personal belongings were in his barracks bag, which was left at his company's headquarters. The men carried a backpack that included only a rolled-up blanket, a sleeping bag, a rifle, ammo, and a small pick and shovel that would get a lot of use. They lived mostly in foxholes during much of this time. He remembered it was very muddy in Italy. "We marched up one hill and down another, all day and all night to catch up with the Germans as they were quickly retreating." More than seventy years later, he still has the pick he used to dig those foxholes.

During the Battle of San Pietro, DiSalvo was taking cover behind a wall during extremely heavy enemy fire when he felt a sharp pain in his right shoulder. He had taken a hit of shrapnel and needed immediate attention. He was sent back for surgery and then on to the 106th Station Hospital for a week of recovery before revisiting the repo-depo. DiSalvo was awarded a Purple Heart for the wound he sustained during that battle. He then rejoined his outfit as they returned from Rome. By then, his outfit had just captured San Pietro and Monte Cassino.

Meanwhile, back home in the States, DiSalvo's family was notified by telegram that he was wounded and missing in action. His sister went to the Red Cross for help in locating him. When they couldn't help her, she enlisted the help of Senator George Stanton, and he was able to locate DiSalvo, giving his family a great sense of relief. DiSalvo had also received a telegram from Senator Stanton's office while recuperating, explaining his family's dilemma. "There was so many of us wounded or killed, it must have been impossible to keep track of," he said.

While recovering at the repo-depo, DiSalvo requested and was granted KP duty, peeling potatoes for the troops. Being on KP meant he would also get a pass to go into town once in a while. He loved the Italian food and enjoyed being able to find some normalcy during the crazy wartime battles. He vividly remembered serving stew to the soldiers during his time doing KP. In line were more of his old pals from Fitchburg—Salvator "Suitcase" Lunetta, Patsy Sardo, Merl Perry, Vito Testagrossa, Sam Ricciuti, and many others—all part of the Twenty-Sixth Division that was sent in as replacements.

According to DiSalvo's memory, "The Battle for San Pietro had consisted of the Third Division, the Thirty-Sixth, and the Forty-Fifth Divisions." After the area had been secured and the divisions were able to advance, DiSalvo and company were assigned more training. "We were being trained for an invasion into southern France."

The Allied D-day invasion into Normandy had started on June 6, 1944. This was all or none, win or lose, and the war's outcome would be determined by this strategic move for the Allies to get onto Axis soil from the west. However, with Overlord casualties mounting for the Allies and forces being bogged down in the hedgerows of Normandy, Anvil was needed to draw the Germans elsewhere. Operation Anvil was originally planned as a simultaneous invasion to Overlord but didn't occur until two months later. By August 1944, "We were practicing for the landings for southern France, using LSTs and LCIs. Run down the plank, into the water and onto the shore," said DiSalvo. The Seventh Army, Sixth Corps, including DiSalvo's Third Division and the Thirty-Sixth and Forty-Fifth, were loaded up and headed for France.

Chapter 4

⭐

Life Saving, Life Changing

There were LSTs full of troops departing from Salerno, Italy, to Marseille, in France. Fighting was ferocious, and the LSTs didn't provide much cover. Once on French soil, the troops would regroup and push deeper into France. The Allies who were on the west coast had been under tremendous fire, and this group was no different. "There was always resistance," DiSalvo said. "We'd be in tanks or trucks, chasing them. We'd stop, start fighting again, and keep pushing north." DiSalvo's troops moved under heavy fire into a town in southern France called Marseille, just west of Monaco. He remembered riding on a tank in Marseille; the roads and ride were so tough, they almost rocked him off.

The winter in France was a cold one. "At night, we'd stop to rest. We had sleeping bags with us and everything, and the big heavy army coats they gave us. We'd just lie down and cover up. We'd wake up and have three inches of snow covering our bodies. We were on the ground. We didn't pitch tents."

On December 8, 1944, DiSalvo literally saved the life of one of his wounded mates. "One of my men was in the foxhole with me. It was another situation of shooting at one another across a field. We were standing up and shooting at the enemy, and I felt something. I turned around and looked at my partner. 'What's the matter?' I asked him. 'Did

188

you get hit?' He said, 'Yeah, I got shot.' I didn't know it, you know, so I pulled him back down into the foxhole. We all carried a first-aid kit, so I broke open the powder and put it on him, stopped the bleeding, and bandaged him up. But there was no place I could bring him at first." Fortunately, the German troops they were fighting soon surrendered. "I called for a medic—you know, 'Come over and take this guy.' They put him on a stretcher and took him away. I never heard from the guy and figured he went home. He never came back to the outfit. I never heard from him again." Many years later, DiSalvo discovered the man's name was William Howard and that he was alive and well, living in North Carolina.

Almost seventy years later, an amazing online thread showed up from the Texas Military Forces Museum. It read, in part, as follows:

> My father served with Sgt. DiSalvo. I believe Sgt. DiSalvo was a Sgt. in one of the rifle platoons of "G" company of the 143rd Infantry Regiment (2nd Battalion). My father was in the weapons platoon of Company "G." On or around December 8th, 1944 my father was wounded by a mortar blast, and due to blood and debris in his eyes, he could not see. He was stumbling around on a hillside in a very dangerous situation with Germans attacking and mortars landing, without the ability to see where he was going. I am almost positive it was Sgt. DiSalvo who left his foxhole to guide my father to safety in his (Sgt. DiSalvo's) foxhole. My father is still alive and I will ask him for details on Sgt. DiSalvo and post them here. Please tell Sgt. DiSalvo's niece to give her uncle a hug for both my father and for myself and our family. It is quite possible my father would not be here w/o his act of courage.

Best wishes, John W. Howard, son of William M. Howard G/143

There was more.

Santo DiSalvo was indeed the person who pulled my father into his foxhole and called for a medic when my father was wounded. One of the things my father remembers about Mr. DiSalvo is the fact that his (DiSalvo's) Thompson SMG was almost taller than he was![28]

DiSalvo commented emotionally on this article. "His son was looking for me." He paused to collect his thoughts of that day. "He wanted to find me and thank me for saving his father's life. I never thought of it that way. He wanted me to know his father was still living and that I saved his life."

COURAGE UNDER FIRE

The Distinguished Service Cross: December 18, 1944.

> The act or acts of heroism use have been so notable and have involved risk of life so extraordinary as to set the individual apart from his or her comrades.
>
> The President of the United States takes pleasure in presenting the Distinguished Service Cross to Santo J. DiSalvo, Private First Class, U.S. Army, for extraordinary heroism in connection with military operations against an armed enemy while serving

---

28 http://valor.militarytimes.com/recipient.php?recipientid=30768.

with Company G, 143d Infantry Regiment, 36th Infantry Division, in action against enemy forces on 18 December 1944. When his squad was pinned down by heavy enemy fire, Private First Class DiSalvo, by rising, drew all enemy fire upon himself, enabling his men to withdraw to cover. Then, although a target for enemy machine gun fire, he single-handedly captured the enemy emplacement. Headquarters, Seventh U.S. Army, General Orders No. 258 (1945).

DiSalvo gave an amazing effort to get that job done. His accounts of that day are courageous by anyone's standards. "We were pinned down and couldn't move. Something had to be done. Then the following day, we were able to move forward. The machine guns were gone," he said with quiet modesty. "They were in the woods and we were pinned down in a grape vineyard. We couldn't go anywhere until we stopped that machine gun. I never expected to get anything for it. It ain't why I did it. You know, a war's a war." Seventy years later, DiSalvo remembered the details vividly. He stared back to a place long ago and shook his head. "They're shooting at you, you shoot at them. I was surprised when my platoon sergeant wrote me up." He continued, "He wrote me up for a Silver Star, but headquarters thought it deserved more."

Months later, on a clear spring day in 1945, DiSalvo was awarded the nation's second-highest honor, the Distinguished Service Cross. "The whole regiment was there, all lined up in the field. A bunch of us were getting medals, standing at attention. A general was there to pin them on us. There was a band and everything; it was a big affair. The war wasn't over yet." Thirty-eight members of the 143rd Infantry Regiment went on to receive the prestigious Distinguished Service Cross. According to homeofheroes.com, only four thousand would be handed out during the entire war. There were 16.5 million US soldiers who participated during that period of time.[29,30]

The Distinguished Service Cross is awarded to a person who, while serving in any capacity with the army, distinguishes himself or herself by extraordinary heroism not justifying the award of a Medal of Honor; while engaged in an action against an enemy of the United States; while engaged in military operations involving conflict with an opposing/foreign force; or while serving with friendly foreign forces engaged in an armed conflict against an opposing armed force in which the United States is not a belligerent party. The act or acts of heroism must have been so notable and have involved risk of life so extraordinary as to set the individual apart from his or her comrades.

ADVANCING FORWARD: CHASING THE GERMANS

"The Germans were retreating so fast, we had to chase them. We were in trucks, and they were too, shooting at each other through the woods or through a big open field." Throughout France and Germany, they'd battle—get out for a day off, and then go back at it again. He would see his old friends with whom he'd grown up in Fitchburg passing him when they would switch troops on the front line. DiSalvo usually walked with the rest of the troops, shooting and advancing. At times, the roads ahead were clear and all the men piled onto trucks or tanks and rode until there was return fire or an ambush. The men had to get back down and walk, shoot, and advance one foot at a time.

Another amazing feat of DiSalvo's Thirty-Sixth Division was that they held on to the front line for 210 days. He remembered hearing that they may have held a record for holding the front line as a division longer than any other on the Germany/France line—seven months of

---

29 http://www.homeofheroes.c.../03_wwii-dsc/army_d.html.
30 https://en.m.wikipedia.org/wiki/143rd_Infantry_Regiment_(United_States).

constant under-fire. He explained how they got one day off, maybe two, but usually one, during which they'd walk back beyond the line of battle and rest, eat, or whatever. Their replacements would pass them on their way to the battle line after their "day off." They'd relieve each other's company as part of the overall Thirty-Sixth Division.

DiSalvo said the Germans knew about the Allies' guns and other weapons. "When we had prisoners, they'd look at it. They knew it made a big hole when it came out. A .45 bullet, once it explodes, it goes in but tears a big hole in the body when it comes out. They were afraid of that .45," DiSalvo said, shaking his head with the trace of a smirk.

Chapter 5

Keep Chasing Nazis

From France, DiSalvo went into Germany, just about three miles outside of Hamburg, to one of the US headquarters. They took a train into Hamburg. The city was demolished, as was Frankfurt. "They were a mess," DiSalvo said. Nonetheless, he said, the American soldiers were met with little hostility from most German citizens. "The only ones that would give you a mean look and a stare were the hardcore Nazis. The regular people were fine. We got along good with them." While in Germany, DiSalvo was promoted from buck sergeant to staff sergeant. "They were losing men so fast, promotions came quick." If you had a field commission, you had to go to school. If you failed, you were demoted to a private.

He was placed in charge of a squad of about fifteen men. Part of the staff sergeant's responsibilities was to order his squad where they needed to go. There were usually three or four squads per platoon. DiSalvo was in the Third Platoon, Third Squad.

As a result of promotions, DiSalvo and a few other soldiers needed to have their new stripes sewed on their uniforms. They asked around and found a woman who was not a die-hard Nazi and could sew. She was afraid of the Nazis, DiSalvo said. The soldiers had to reassure her that she would be protected—that once they left that area, another company would come in after them and control the headquarters there.

In Germany, HQ found billets for them to stay in. The whole town was full of American soldiers, he recalled. "They had this big bin of potatoes in the house we stayed in. There were six of us in one house." The food was horrible, and they craved good cooking. "Everyone was out there trading cigarettes for eggs because our rations were awful. All we had was mutton for lunch and dinner. We got to hate mutton real quick." A bunch of the soldiers planned their own operation to get rid of the mutton. They secretly agreed to "go back for seconds and thirds and just throw it out to get rid of it. They had so much of it, they would have fed it to us for months." He laughed. "The K rations were better, but the C rations in the cans—maybe one was worth eating, but they were awful."

As they moved from Germany to Austria, there was, as always plenty of resistance and return fire. The Germans were almost finished, but not quite yet. While DiSalvo was in Austria, word got out that Germany had surrendered and the war in Europe would soon be coming to a close. "There were some storm troopers, the SS, up on a hill," DiSalvo said. "They wouldn't surrender unless we let them keep their guns. There was no way we were going to let them keep their guns. We finally got them down and there was a big stockade for them. We used to have to pull guard duty ... They'd look up at us and snarl. They were the mean bastards. They even killed their own men ... They'd come in and give them all orders. The regular men didn't want to be in that war any more than we did."

Whenever they pulled back from the line, they'd find a place to stay for a night or two. They would take over a home and ask the owners if they'd cook a meal for them, offering to pay for it. He remembered meeting a little girl and asking her if she knew anyone who could cook for them. She said she did. They'd been at an old farmer's house that had dirt floors. This was, after all, wartime in the mid-1940s, there she cooked pasta and beans. He loved it: good, healthful, warm food. They had hot water, which the men used to shave and bathe properly. The following morning, before leaving, they cooked a breakfast of potatoes and eggs. "In Austria, finding food wasn't so easy. Most people wouldn't cook for us."

On the way, the troops moved forward and took over entire towns one at a time. Whenever they took over a town, the rear echelon troops would come in behind them, keeping it Allied occupied while moving troops through.

On May 8, 1945, after 16.5 million men fought the toughest battle known to humankind, Germany surrendered unconditionally, and the war in Europe was finally over. DiSalvo came home to US soil in September 1945. The return boat trip to New York wasn't a picnic, but at least they were heading in the right direction. The weather was horrible nine out of the ten days it took them to return. He remembered staying on the top deck of the ship with another soldier from Hawaii to avoid getting sick. Everyone else around them was suffering from severe seasickness. At most, he got an apple to eat, but so many passengers were leaning over the rails that he didn't have much of an appetite.

He was given a month furlough before having to report back to Fort Devens to be discharged from his service to the United States Army. Staff Sergeant Santo J. DiSalvo was officially discharged on November 23, 1945, at the age of twenty-three and was now a civilian.

After being discharged in Fort Devens, DiSalvo walked the ten-plus miles from the base to his family home in Fitchburg. He wasn't able to write his parents about coming home, and there were no phones for him to make a call, so he just showed up and surprised them. When he came home, his dad opened a special twelve-year-old bottle of Marsala wine he'd been saving for a special occasion. This was one indeed. While DiSalvo was away, he had had his war pay sent home to his family. He was paid $110 month to fight for his country—$10 of which he had kept for whatever he might be able to spend it on.

Home Sweet Home

B eing home meant getting back to work, as well as some normalcy and even a family life. DiSalvo first went to work for Selig Manufactory Company in Leominster, where he stayed for fifteen months. He then went to work for a construction company for a short time.

In November 1947, Clare Angelini and Santo J. DiSalvo were married. The two had met through her sister before he left for war. She'd written to him while he was away, telling him what she'd done, what was happening in town, and making other small talk. They were married for sixty-six years. Clare was eighty-eight years old when she passed away. DiSalvo still has her precious letters to this day. One can only imagine the strength and courage he felt upon receiving her letters during those difficult times so far away from home. Together, they had two loving daughters, Linda and Carol Ann.

In 1954, DiSalvo was appointed as a firefighter for the city of Fitchburg. He retired in June 1985 after thirty-one years of continuing to protect the public and keep them safe. After his retirement, he and Clare traveled the United States and decided where and how to settle down. In the winters, they lived in Arizona, and in the summer, they stayed at a cottage they bought in Maine. Although it was a 2,800-mile trip one way between their two homes, DiSalvo would drive them. DiSalvo drove his own car well into his late eighties.

During World War II, the United States awarded just over five thousand Distinguished Service Cross awards. As a result of DiSalvo's heroic efforts as described above and subsequent DSC award, he is a member of the prestigious and elite Legion of Valor of the United States. Only recipients of the nation's top awards are inducted. Each year, an annual convention is held for the Legion of Valor. None have been missed since the founding in 1890. The headquarters and a museum are in Southern California.

Decades ago, DiSalvo attended a meeting at a farm in South Hamilton, Massachusetts. It was the home of the late General George S. Patton's son, Major General George S. Patton, also a DSC award recipient, who hosted the event. DiSalvo remembered much of the memorabilia decorating the walls and ceilings of Patton's farm. He must have felt very proud to be in the home of such a great leader during World War II.

There are not enough words to describe the kind of gratitude the American people have for such men as Santo J. DiSalvo. So we will use just two—thank you.

DiSanto on right

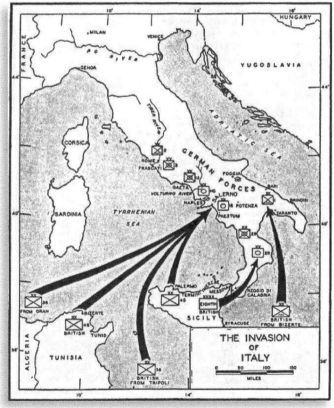

DiSalvo's Invasion was from Oran (far left) to Salerno.

SANTO DISALVO RETURNS BACK HOME AFTER THE WAR.

SANTO DISALVO'S DISTINGUISHED SERVICE CROSS, PURPLE
HEART, RIBBONS AND BADGES HE STILL PROUDLY DISPLAYED.

DiSalvo in Italy.

DiSalvo (center) with fellow soldiers.

DiSalvo PROUDLY STILL HAS HIS DOG TAGS, HIS
TRUSTY SHOVEL AND ALL HIS WAR MEDALS.

UNDATED PHOTO OF SOLDIERS ON A LST.

Amazing destruction.

San Pietro village, far right.

Book 8

TECH SERGEANT JOSEPH R. CHIMINIELLO

Chapter 1

I Don't Know How We Made It

J oseph R. Chiminiello was born December 6, 1925, in Quincy, Massachusetts, the son of Dominic and Madeline (Pecce) Chiminiello. His father emigrated from Italy when he was only three years old; his mother was born in the United States. He had one brother and one sister. His brother, Robert, was not in the military service, and neither was his sister, Camella.

Joseph remembered how they took photos before he went into the service, how on one Sunday afternoon the family gathered around for a rare full-family portrait.

Chiminiello graduated from high school in Quincy. The military service actually allowed him to postpone active duty so he could finish high school. He really enjoyed studying aerodynamics while in high school; little did he know what was in store for him.

He worked with his father in a shipyard, building aircraft carriers. He remembered hearing about the bombing of Pearl Harbor while at work. "This will all blow over," the old man said. "It won't be long." Joseph clearly remembered the soldiers patrolling the beaches of Massachusetts and the coastline after the war had started. "The soldiers were coming down the beach as long as no submarines were coming around," he explained. His father invited the men in uniform in for a drink now and then. The German naval forces were attacking

US ships regularly as the United States attempted to take supplies to England. Unbeknownst to most of the country, German U-boats were sitting off the coastline waiting for the supply ships to come out. From mid-January through August 1942, the German U-boats had strong control of the Eastern Seaboard of the United States. Between February and May of that year, 348 ships were sunk and only two U-boats were lost—sinking more than 3.1 million tons of supplies. The United States instituted "dim-outs" on the coast to prevent the ships' silhouettes from showing their locations against the bright lights of American cities and towns.

The Perini Corporation, for which Chiminiello and his father worked, built a total of seven aircraft carriers. He and his father went up to watch them launch the enormous ships. The senior Chiminiello was a very humble man and taught his son Joseph to be the same way. "He didn't want to show himself as a big deal, but he was a big deal," Joseph Chiminiello said. "We used to go up on the stand and watch them crash the bottle of champagne, and down went the ship. Aircraft carriers ... 888 feet long. I'll never forget that." He was a young, impressionable kid and was amazed by the ingenuity of it all. "They'd say, 'Let's get Joe and show him the carrier.'" He remembered details of even the incredible ductwork needed to get the airflow down the ship.

Chiminiello enlisted with the US Army on November 12, 1943. His terms of enlistment, according to military records, were as follows: "Enlistment for the duration of the war or other emergency, plus six months, subject to the discretion of the president or otherwise according to law."

On March 14, 1944, Chiminiello was officially inducted into the US Army at Fort Devens, Massachusetts. From there, he was sent to Greensboro, North Carolina, and Charlestown, South Carolina, for training—finally ending up in Tyndall Field, Florida, for gunnery training. Originally starting as an aviation cadet, he was eventually assigned as a gunner. "I was good," he said, smiling, "real good."

He loved going to gunnery school and loved being good at his task. At first, they practiced by having trucks drive figure eights around pylons. The gunners were to shoot at targets while moving. "I never missed one," he said proudly during our meeting seventy years later.

He remembered they were tough on the new recruits, requiring the men to make their bunks so tight that the officer could toss a quarter on it and have it bounce. "One time, they came by to see who they would give credit to and for what. There was a bunk on the top and bottom [of the bunk beds]. The officers were looking for tightly made beds. They gave me credit. But it wasn't me, it was the guy up above," he admitted, laughing.

In Tyndall Field, the barracks had belonged to the Women's Army Corps, so they had bathtubs in them. Of course, the tubs didn't get much use from the men.

Chapter 2

Overseas and Living underneath Bombers

O n November 3, 1944, Chiminiello went from New York to Liverpool, England, riding high in the *Queen Mary*. "It was beautiful. I had the ride of my life. My father was a shipbuilder. I was in the aft deck; all I had to do was walk out and get on the backside of the ship. I had to duck when the waves came over me. But the bow of the *Queen Mary* was right in the water. I loved it." He remembered heading into Liverpool and seeing the huge barrage of balloons protecting the ships from enemy strafing. It was a preview of the war to come for the nineteen-year-old Chiminiello.

Joseph Chiminiello was part of the United States Army Air Force, Eighth Army, 389th Bomb Group, in Hethel, England. He was assigned in the "low ball," low turret of a B-17 Flying Fortress and then into the B-24 Liberator. Both bombers were heavily used in the European theater. The aircraft were generally equipped with three turrets: at the top, at the rear, and at the bottom. The place for the bottom turret gunner—Chiminiello's assignment—was a lonesome spot. He was below the ship and without his comrades close by. He was able to see 360 degrees around and under the ship by moving the turret (as described below in detail). Chiminiello fired his dual 50 mm guns at enemy aircraft coming at the bomber from below as they charged up at them.

He usually flew in the B-24 nicknamed *Stork Club*, a name given to it by the pilot, who had family ties to the famous club of the same name in New York City.

"The Sperry lower ball turret was used in the Boeing B-17 Flying fortress and the Consolidated B-24 Liberator. The ball turret was mounted underneath the aircraft and was used to defend the bomber against aircraft attacking from below.

The turret mounted two Browning 50 caliber machine guns that would fire 750 to 850 bullets in a minute, that's about 14 bullets a second. Statistically, the ball turret was one of the safest crew positions during WWII as ball turret gunners had the lowest loss rate.

To get in the turret the gunner would manually crank the guns straight down after take off. He could then open the hatch and would climb in. Once inside he could turn on the turrets electrical and hydraulic power. The gunner would lie inside the turret in a fetal position and would sight between his legs through the circular glass. The turret was powered by an electric motor that drove two Vickers hydraulic units. One for azimuth (sideways) and one for elevation (up and down). The gunner had two handles to control the turret with. On top of these handles were the buttons for firing the guns.

Since the B-24 had very low ground clearance, a retracting mechanism was used to raise and lower the turret for take off and landing."[31]

In all of the war, there were 18,482 B-24s built. The B-24 was produced on a large scale, with almost nineteen thousand units being manufactured across a number of versions. Production took place at five plants. At one time, one B-24 was being produced every hundred minutes, a rate so great that production exceeded the military's ability

---

31 Taigh Ramey, www.Twinbeech.com. October 2016.

to use the aircraft. Such were the production numbers that it has been said that more aluminum, aircrew, and effort went into the B-24 than any other aircraft in history. The logistics of yet another war endeavor are simply staggering.

Chiminiello laughed as he recalled his place in the plane. "I was all rolled into a ball," he said. "I had the best view. All I had to do was turn it and look around." At 5 feet 6 inches and weighing in at 140 pounds, Chiminiello learned how to squeeze into the ball turret and sit there for hours and hours. On getting into the turret, he explained, "You turn it, get in, press a few buttons, and you're down." He was switched from a B-17 to a B-24; the B-24 was a much different aircraft for the aircrew. They learned a lot about flying in a war in that B-24. He remembered how the turret would go up and down into the fuselage, and how he had to learn how to get in and out of it from inside the fuselage. "When that turret went down, I didn't know if I was going out of the ship." Seven decades later, he laughed about this dangerous act. "Then we went up into the ship so we could get out of the turret. Just the opposite, but you had to get into position."

Looking out his window as he remembered a place far away from his comfortable home, he said, "The B-24 ... Jesus mackerel, what a plane." Then, "We lost a lot of guys," he said solemnly. Unlike some of the turret gunners, Chiminiello had two parachutes with him: "one on the belly and one on the back. I was going to make sure I was going to live." Referring to the parachutes, he added, "There were only us three!

"The B-24 was a good ship; it did the job for us. We were lucky. That plane was butchered," he said, recalling the condition of the *Stork Club* returning from missions.

Along with Chiminiello, there were three other men from New England in the *Stork Club*. They were from Troy, New York; Lexington, Massachusetts; and Lowell, Massachusetts. They formed a strong kinship. From Chiminiello's personal notes is a list of some of his crew:

Pilot Lieutenant Howard Sloan
Pilot Lieutenant Malcolm W. Levi
Bombardier Tech Sergeant Ward H. Powers
Navigator Lieutenant Charles Troy
Top gunner Staff Sergeant Ora M. Price
Waist gunner Staff Sergeant Robert Martin
Waist gunner Staff Sergeant Donald G. Pierce
Tail gunner Staff Sergeant James F. Leonard

Chapter 3

Plenty of Instances to Have Been Killed

Chiminiello was lucky that he had his own camera and was able to take lots of photos. He often mused that his own guys might think he was a spy. "When the planes were coming back," he said, pausing to collect his memories, "some of them dead. I'd go down the field every day too … to make sure, you know, that they were all coming back." He further explained, "I had my own bicycle and would ride down to the field to make sure my plane came back. We didn't always have the same planes. They were down for maintenance or something. But we always had the same crew, all the time."

Like many of the airfields during the war, theirs had a larger runway for distressed aircraft, wider and longer than the others. If a plane was all shot up and damaged, it would use a different runway, where it was hoped that the extra space would allow a safe landing. Chiminiello remembered his crew needing to use that runway. "We had a wheel shot off. I had to leave the turret and go into the fuselage. With both [landing] gears down, the left one was shot to hell. They landed and it went *blub, blub, blub, blub*. We had champ pilots." He nodded. "We had holes in the plane … What the hell, everyone had holes in their plane. One plane was showing with two-hundred-plus fragmentations in it … The guys made it. Not one got hurt."

Once they were airborne, one of Chiminiello's duties was to arm the bombs. "You never knew what you were gonna carry. We could carry four one-ton bombs in a B-24. I used to pull the pins after you take off, then they're armed. You go back to your position and that was it." Chiminiello thought he had a very advantageous position in the aircraft. "If you keep moving, they wouldn't bother you. That was the whole secret. Keep moving the turret. They [the enemy] saw that moving. They knew you were alert."

There were regular problems. At altitudes, the temperatures were frigid, decreasing by about 4.5 degrees per thousand feet of climb. Heated suits were commonplace by that time, but they were far from perfect. "It was 27 degrees below zero [Fahrenheit]; my right rubber boot wasn't heating," Chiminiello said. "I kept knocking it on the side of the ship to keep it warm. Another time it was 58 degrees below zero, in the middle of winter." The combination of the extreme cold, needing to use oxygen to stay alive, being alone in the turret bubble, watching 360 degrees around the bottom of the aircraft for oncoming enemy, and having two 50 mm guns at his fingertips was quickly making a man out of the young Chiminiello. These missions were a common occurrence. It was his job, and he was proud that he did it well.

His crew would regularly fly at twenty-seven thousand feet. Other aircraft were at staggered altitudes around thirty thousand feet. "They [the other American bomber planes] would bomb us too. If you both get to the target at the same time, you drop them anyway. It was crazy. You felt bad for the flights that were going down. The formations were nine, ten, eleven; it was supposed to be twelve, but it all depends on who gets up there and who's where. I don't think we ever managed ten or twelve planes."

Although they wanted to look like a tight squadron from the ground, the formation flew too close for his comfort. "We'd have to pull a gun on them to get them away. They were too close. They were only showing off, and it was too close." The B-17s were over twenty-seven thousand feet; the B-24s were lower. Sometimes the B-17s' bombs would actually drop onto the B-24s that were beneath them. "We'd just cross our fingers; there was nothing else to do."

On occasion, they'd be lucky to have an escort. "Once in a while the P-51 [Mustang fighter ship] would be there. They'd be high, or he'd pull right up to me and we'd wave." They didn't get their help all the time. "But they were great. We loved them."

Chiminiello remembered certain details of several missions. "Yeah, I remember it like it was yesterday," he said, more to himself than to me. "We were in formation. One plane was hit. The wing fell right off the plane. It was shot and folded right up. One of the guys was burned really badly and got thrown out of the ship. He was the only one. The B-24, you don't get out of it—that's the idea. If you're lucky, you make it; you had to be [in a] damn good position. You either got thrown out or something. You do carry the chutes; we'd see a few go down. The idea was to count them, see who's gone and who isn't gone. But most of the time, the B-24 wasn't the safest ship."

Another mission had 1,500 planes in it. Seven hundred were B-17s and were, as usual, above the eight hundred B-24s. "Boy, it looked good—for a while, anyway. Until the pursuit ships had some fun with it. I had one I chased off. It was a nose deal where he's approaching you at four hundred miles per hour. We're at three hundred miles per hour, so that's coming fast on the nose. Very fast ... 500 shells per turret ... 550 shells exactly." Chiminiello loved the job he was assigned. He enjoyed being a good shooter.

He also was a friend of the famed actor Jimmy Stewart. "I knew him. He was a commander. He flew twenty missions. I didn't fly with him though. We got scrubbed one time so he could go to Berlin after it was pulverized. I used to rub him about that one. He'd tell us, 'We'll be all right. We're gonna come back and all meet right here.' He took a B-24 just over the ground one time. They wanted to know who was strafing so close, showing off [his piloting skills]. They all knew who it was, but no one would rat on him. "But we all knew who it was."

Some great entertainers visited them. Chiminiello remembered seeing James Cagney visit the troops. The war effort was truly a full effort put forth by the United States and its industries, especially the movie studios, who helped keep morale high.

They had two long missions, Chiminiello recalled, one to Austria and another to Poland. "Twelve hundred miles each way. Those were bad. Weather was cold as hell. Twelve hours per trip. We'd get a tankful of fuel that would take us. I sometimes wondered where they got all the gas. We didn't eat, we didn't do anything, and we just flew. They gave us three pieces of candy. I could see the war going on down below. We could see the land. I had to keep the turret moving. There was one that was going to come after me, but I showed him I was awake and a sharpshooter. It didn't matter to me what he did. The sights had a line in them. You could frame the plane coming in." From his position in the turret, he'd make sure all the bombs would drop properly. He'd watch them fall far below on their targets.

Another mission ended tragically for many in his formation. "One guy got hit by Germans. He hit the plane and then he [the plane that was hit] hit the lead ship, jumped up and hit the deputy lead, and jumped up and hit the lead of the next group. One guy took out four ships, forty men. You don't get out of the 24. It was tough." He confessed, "The turret is not the safest place to be when the ship is going down. You just don't get out. It's a horrible place to be.

"The weather there was bad, very bad. Lots of times, we'd get into formation and all you could see was the underbelly of the other planes. All you could see was under. The pilots couldn't even see. It was all foggy. When you get the weather [briefings], you don't know for sure what you'll get until you get there."

Throughout the interview, Chiminiello sounded like a typical young kid at the time. He was not afraid of anything; it was as though nothing could hurt him. Others might get hurt, maybe, but he was sure he'd survive—from his little space in the turret where he enjoyed the view he'd always remember. What others might have deemed catastrophic problems were minor inconveniences to this kid. He just kept it moving and shot with deadly accuracy.

He remembered how they very seldom flew at night. They'd get up early and come back very late. By this time, night flying in formation—in the clouds, rain, snow, fog, just bad weather, and being attacked with flak—had been established as more hazardous than daytime bombing raids.

Chapter 4

Hardly Rested between Bombings

Chiminiello and crew flew twenty-eight missions before their first leave. "That was bad. I didn't like that, but they wanted to get the war over with." He flew a total of thirty missions as required and was released on April 21, 1945. "We were a very lucky crew." Three weeks before the war ended, Chiminiello finished his tour of duty. He was in London celebrating when they heard Germany had surrendered. If needed, he was ready to go to Japan on the B-29s.

In total, Chiminiello's flying calendar was quite full. Here's a partial list from his records:

1944—December 23, 24, 27
1945—January 2, 3, 29
February 3, 6, 14, 22, 27
March 9, 10, 12, 23, 30
April 7, 10, 11, 14, 16, 17, 21

Upon returning to the States, Chiminiello immediately became ill with a high fever of over 110 and was admitted to a hospital in Florida for more than four weeks. His condition was mostly attributed to "battle fatigue."

Upon returning, he admitted, "I dropped away. I never got interested in the war anymore. Later, they were kind of talking about it more. I'd like to forget the damn thing." Chiminiello continued, "When we came home, no one ever questioned us … what we put up with, what we did. That was a stunner. Like there was no war."

Chiminiello married a few years after returning home. His blessings were his beautiful family: Joseph Jr., Donna, Michele, Jeannine, Joan, and Charles. Also upon returning, Chiminiello went to work with his father again in shipbuilding, where he rose to a supervisory position in a career he loved. He took pride in always treating people equally. He retired as a superintendent for the Perini Corporation.

Chiminiello and I met for this interview on December 16, 2015. He passed away peacefully on January 20, 2016. Thank you, Sergeant Chiminiello, for the years of your youth that you dedicated to the United States and the free world.

CHIMINIELLO ON HIS BIKE TO CHECK ON
RETURNING TROOPS FROM BATTLE.

CHIMINIELLO SMILING AFTER ANOTHER RIDE TO THE
RUNWAYS, THIS TIME ALL RETURNED SAFELY.

CHIMINIELLO'S *STORK CLUB*. KNEELING SECOND R-L.

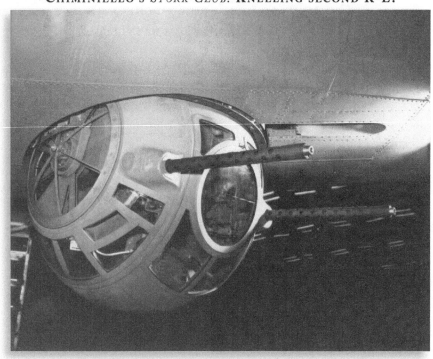

BALL TURRET SIMILAR TO CHIMINIELLO'S
FRONT SEAT FOR THE WAR.

THE STORK CLUB B-24.

ON THEIR WAY IN LOOSE FORMATION.

FROM CHIMINIELLO'S VIEW

Book 9

SECOND LIEUTENANT
CHARLES R. ROGERS

Grasshopper Pilot

Charles R. Rogers was born November 7, 1919, in Geneva, New York, to Warren and Emily Rogers. Charles was the eldest child and followed by a brother, Robert, and a sister, Nancy. Charlie was ninety-six years young during our interviews, when he displayed an amazing memory full of great details and a zest for sharing them.

Geneva is in upstate New York in the Finger Lakes region. The Finger Lakes are a group of eleven long, narrow, roughly north-south lakes. They are some of the deepest in the country, and the area is a great tourist vacation spot. Rogers remembered having a good childhood, including some exciting times, such as speedboat races on the lakes. He remembered, as a little boy, purchasing balsa-wood miniature airplanes at local toy stores. You'd have to assemble them, and the prop would spin based on how tight you'd twisted the elastic band beneath the little fuselage.

On Saturday mornings, Rogers would head to the local corner store to look through the comic books. With the likes of Doc Savage and the Shadow, his favorites were the ones featuring the warbirds of World War I, all types of Fokkers, and the Red Baron. Is that what determined his future?

His father sold insurance in Geneva and was actually a three-time mayor of the city. His mom grew up on a farm in northern Pennsylvania and was a great influence on them all. They simply accepted the Depression. They didn't complain about how things were; they were content just living day to day. The problems in Europe didn't include the Rogers family—not yet anyway.

Interestingly, Charles's brother, Robert, was a member of the Marine ROTC before the war started. He served during World War II in the South Pacific and rose to be a captain in the US Marine Corps. In 1942, Robert Harding Rogers was on active military duty in the United States Marine Corps, Company E, Eighth Marines, Second Division. Robert Rogers served in five campaigns in the South Pacific; while in Guadalcanal, he was wounded and awarded the Purple Heart. In 1943, Robert was promoted to Rifle Company Commander and led his troops in the Tarawa campaign, the first American offensive in the critical central Pacific region and one of the deadliest battles of World War II. Then, in 1944, Robert served as captain in the Saipan campaign, after which he was awarded the Silver Star for his inspiring leadership, tactical judgment, and zealous devotion to duty. Robert also served as Rifle Company commander officer during the Tinian and Okinawa campaigns. In 1945, Robert Rogers was honored with the Bronze Star for meritorious achievement as Rifle Company commander of Company E from 1942 to 1945. This family has achieved many great accomplishments, ones to be extremely proud of.

Charlie Rogers graduated from Geneva High School in 1938. During high school times, Rogers may have been aware of world affairs, but he was more interested in his daily high school life than Nazi Germany's movement. It would be a few more years before the news coverage was extensive enough to catch his attention. Rogers loved to draw in high school, and entertained himself by drawing his fellow classmates and schoolteachers. It was no surprise that after high school he attended the Rochester Institute of Technology, Rochester Art School and later became a commercial artist.

When the Japanese attacked Pearl Harbor on December 7, 1941, Rogers remembered, he had been hitchhiking home from school and arrived that afternoon. His father met him at the door and told him about the Pearl Harbor attack. Rogers immediately decided he would have to enlist in the armed services. He knew they had a recruiting office in downtown Rochester, and upon his return on Monday, he enlisted in the US Armed Forces. Originally, he tried to sign up for the marines, but he was informed he was too short; he received the same answer from the navy. Finally, he ended up with the US Army.

He was instructed to be ready to leave by train within two weeks. The group of enlistments had him worried about his choice; they included only five other farmhands—including two scared brothers who were holding hands. The rest of his friends from the RIT signed up for ground crews with the army air corps.

Once in boot camp, he was sent to Camp Upton on the tip of Long Island for a week. His first training in weaponry was supposed to be with 105 mm guns. However, he used a 240 mm gun having the sound and feel of a Howitzer cannon. He actually enjoyed basic training and learning how to march in the military; full gun classes included taking the guns apart and putting them back together, even in the dark. There were also many other types of shooting competitions. Rogers figured he impressed someone with his gun handling, because he was the second of his group to go to officer candidate school. The OCS was in Fort Sill, Oklahoma, where he was promoted to second lieutenant. This was his first time away from home. He did, however, have a five-day leave between the two stops to go home for a short visit before heading off to the war in Europe.

Chapter 2

Officer Candidate School

HIS TWO LOVES: MARY AND A PIPER CUB

Rogers was in OCS for three months and enjoyed that portion of his training as well. It was very organized, and he was learning the officer's military way, like how to issue commands and project his voice properly. The schools ran very rapidly and demanded the best of a soldier. Although only 50 percent eventually graduated, Rogers was a smart and skilled student, making him one of the lucky ones.

Rogers applied for and was granted further training at Pine Camp in upstate New York and was there from July 1942 until early November 1942. He was now part of the Fourth Armored Division, General Patton's division. Rogers was trained for several different positions. "One was as a forward observer to adjust artillery guns on a target," he said years later.

Charlie Rogers was nicknamed Buck after the futuristic comic book star Buck Rogers. During one of the training exercises in Tennessee, the group was traveling through some backwoods; Rogers was in charge of the ammunition train, with ten half-track vehicles assigned to go and retrieve artillery shells. At some point, Rogers's captain shouted, "Hey, Buck, put Lieutenant Wiseman in charge of the ammunition train and you get in with me and help me check the column." (A *column* is a convoy of vehicles.) Lieutenant Wiseman had been with the group only one month and was a fairly new lieutenant. In only ten minutes, Rogers got a taste of the luck and loss of war. The half-track Rogers had just left for Wiseman was forced to pull over to let another vehicle pass by. The half-track slipped and cascaded forty feet down a bank, falling on its top and killing six men—including Rogers's replacement, Lieutenant Wiseman.

During the winter, they went to California's Mohave Desert for additional training. It was very hot and very dry and had strong dust storms, making visibility near zero. In May 1943, Rogers was given leave to go back home to Geneva, New York. While there, he and Mary Connors were married on May 17. The newly married Rogers quickly returned to the Mohave, where he saw a notice on a bulletin board for artillery officers to learn to fly Piper Cubs as artillery spotter pilots. Rogers signed up and was selected. He was whisked off to Kansas for three months of pilot flight training. Once again, only 50 percent of those training recruits were expected to make the cut, whereas the other half would wash out and be sent to various other specialties. Rogers made the cut as a pilot. "That little plane was part of me," he said. "I could do anything with it."

At first, Rogers was learning to fly an L-3 Taylorcraft Aeronca. He then moved on to the famous L-4 Piper Cub, the little observation and liaison plane nicknamed the Grasshopper. They had tandem seating, front and back, for two—as well as a small engine that would cruise around 65 mph.

For another month, he went on to learn how to fly the Cubs at Fort Sill. His new best friend for life would be the Piper Cub. She didn't really come equipped with much except basic instrumentation: altimeter, airspeed indicator, turn/bank coordinator, RPM gauge, oil pressure and oil temperature gauges, and a compass. There was no electrical system in the little plane. That also meant no electric starter. Someone would have to be outside the aircraft and hand pull the propeller while Rogers was at the controls. He'd prime the engine for some fuel from inside the cockpit, switch the magnetos on, and then, with both brakes on, crack open the throttle about an inch and yell from the cockpit to the prop man, "Contact!" The soldier in front of the prop would use both hands high on one of the propeller blades to pull the prop downward in a fast, hard, clean sweeping motion while stepping backward. If you were the one pulling the prop, you were hoping not to get hit by the descending blade and not to get run over by the aircraft now running with blades turning so fast you couldn't see them. Dust was flying everywhere, forcing you to squint, noise filled your recently quiet head, and there was the smell of gasoline and oil being burned through the short exhaust pipes a foot away from you.

Rogers learned things pilots say you should avoid without specialty training. He learned how to land on dusty and winding country roads and take off again from short roads with plenty of trees and obstructions with his docile Piper Cub. He got training using pontoons that were attached to the plane, and learned how to land and take off in water. Calm water is deceiving and tricky to land and take off on, and still, calm water causes too much drag on the pontoons to take off. And, from low altitudes during landings, it is almost impossible to judge your distance. Rogers explained his technique. "I'd fly low and stir up the water, then turn around and come back to use the turbulent water to land on." Water landing at night was especially difficult. "The moon and stars would reflect off the water. Wait for the tail to hit, add power, then nose forward." This conflicted with his depth perception, with the need to add a touch of power by feel and instinct.

There was some more training in night flying. Rogers recalled the following story. "Being up alone in the Cub, I climbed about two thousand feet up. It was pitch-black. I used to read about World War I warbirds and read about an Immelmann [an aerobatic maneuver that has the pilot do a half loop and then turn to a roll, thereby reversing direction while gaining altitude]. So I dove the plane down to get extra speed, pulled back to climb, but when I got to the top of the loop, the prop stopped. Dead silence in pitch-black. I stared down at the ground and did the only thing I could do … nose down and full power. The engine came back on." It was very common after WWI for young children to grow up hearing stories about the incredible pilots, their maneuvers, and how they saved the day. Not many of those stories were about the ones who were killed doing those same maneuvers. The Piper Cub was never designed for such maneuvers, and Rogers had actually cut off the fuel feed to the carburetor while inverted.

Most of his flights would be just above terrain, hopping just over poles and trees like a giant grasshopper. Rogers learned how to take off from very short fields the hard way. They'd put a rope way out in front of him, and he'd have to climb up over it. As he progressed, the rope would come in closer and closer, making it tougher and tougher for him to climb over it without stalling the aircraft and losing any climb performance.

He also learned how to fly triangle points, finding his way to the three points using a compass and wind correction adjustments as needed. It's very difficult to fly a particular direction at low altitudes; at higher altitudes, a pilot's vision is expanded to see more of the earth beneath him to find his way. Most of Rogers's altitudes were from ten feet to twenty-five feet or just over tree height, all while using only his compass and good eyes and memory. Flying at those points at very low altitudes perfected his basic skill of flying, along with his skill of "dead reckoning."

Rogers was becoming the master of his aircraft and learning "seat-of-the-pants" flying.

Chapter 3

★

Assignment: Overseas

REAL TREETOP FLYING, BUT THEY WANT TO KILL US

C harlie Rogers was now part of the Seventh Army, Forty-Fourth Infantry Division and assigned to a special artillery group for spotting the enemy. While at Camp Croft in South Carolina, he learned he'd be rushed overseas as a replacement pilot. He spent one week in Washington, DC, at Camp Meade and went from there to Boston Harbor with troops of soldiers to be loaded up on the HMS *Aquatania*, also known as *Ship Beautiful*—the second-largest ship in the world at that time—and embarked to France. The convoy's trip lasted five long days, which included time with six men in a cabin. There were a few trips to the rail from seasickness. When they landed, Rogers remembered going down the side of the ship on rope ladders to smaller boats. They loaded that night directly onto a train and went "blackout" through Scotland and to Southampton, in England. He was still a second lieutenant and had the promise of a promotion upon reaching his outfit. It was now late 1944, and thirty pilot replacements were heading to Epinal, in the southeast section of France.

D-day had already occurred months before, with many pilot casualties. The rush was on to get these thirty pilots into the air. Rogers was told to not even unpack his belongings, as they were behind schedule. On a jeep and headed to the front, Rogers was notified the outfit had lost many planes and pilots. The Sauer River was the front line for Rogers; they were staying in a German house with a German family of four. They were given the top floor of the house. Rogers was with his mechanic, two helpers, and two observers.

Rogers also had a passenger, sort of—an observer. The observer was also the one with the radio; he'd make the calls such as where to aim the weapons to fire upon the enemy, as well as make notes of enemy locations.

"One hour goes awfully slow," Rogers said. His first day had him in a jeep heading with his commanding officer to the operations officer, closer to the front. He was then given a full briefing of where the enemy was and the checkpoints. Checkpoints were used on maps to designate where to fire. The division had twelve planes total and a major in charge of the air section. Rogers received his flying missions daily. There were usually three, four, or five missions per day. On just his first mission, Rogers learned how well prepared the German soldiers were. He was fired upon almost immediately and would have to dodge and constantly dive away from enemy fire. They shot everything at them, from the small arms to the big shrapnel firing ground-to-air defense guns known as "ack-ack." The ack-ack would shoot a big orange blast, then change to black clouds and spray the air. Rogers flew over a large open field known as "bellevue." The Germans had zoned in on that field, as well. They had spotters of their own on the ground that calculated Rogers's altitude so the German troops could fire at him more accurately.

Rogers vividly remembered the flak going off all around his plane— under him, over him, and on either side. He could have easily been hit. "I didn't worry about it," said Rogers. "I just made sure I was going up and down like a snake, trying to make sure they didn't have an easy shot. My poor observer was back there calling in anything he could see that we needed to shoot at. The ones we could see the most were the artillery locations. They'd spit out fire and smoke that we could see. The tanks, we saw them and would [have the troops] fire on them with armor-piercing shells. Troops from behind would come up through. Shells would be set for their proximity and would explode in the air just above them and spray them with fragments.

"We'd usually be flying at eight hundred to a thousand feet above them, so we had a good chance [of them hitting us]. They'd shoot everything they had at you. They'd also send Messerschmitts at us, fighter planes. They'd send two—one high and one low. The high one would direct the lower one where we were. You never saw the low one, and that was the one that would shoot you down." That was Rogers's first mission.

Each artillery division had two to three flights per day, with sixteen planes led by a major, a captain, and a first lieutenant. Each plane took one hour at the front. "Going and coming from the front, you'd never use the same direction," Rogers said. "Come in one way, out the other."

The crew of two always used a detailed map of the area during those flights. They'd get it ahead of time during their prebriefing. "It had a lot of details, always had checkpoints that you could see," said Rogers. "Up there at eight hundred, a thousand feet, the map was folded in a two-piece Lucite frame. We'd write over it with a grease pencil, marking our location based on checkpoints. If we were shot down, our orders were to ruin the maps on the way down." He'd then return to the gunners for their fire, telling them where the enemy troops were from his maps.

Rogers talked about flying special missions, but fuel was always an issue. "We could stay up for an hour and a half, maybe a little more." He remembered one very bad day when "they were firing at us so much, the sky was full of the little white popcorn things. It was just full of it. That night we dug foxholes. You couldn't get any sleep. You could hear the gunshots, hear the shells in the air, and hear it hit close to us. Almost zeroed in on us, not close enough, but close enough that your leg would come out of that sleeping bag—you'd get ready to run or something."

Rogers recalled how he had another new observer fly with him for half an hour. When they landed, the observer was actually crying and saying he would not go up again. "He was a big husky guy, football-hero-looking guy," recalled Rogers. He was sent back home, and Rogers was sent flying with a different observer. When I asked Rogers if he was scared, he replied, "You're apprehensive when you're up there and they're breaking all around you, but you had a job to do and that's all you were thinking about. That doing the right job and that your observer would be able to put the right artillery on the people."

His troops didn't have a typical home base. The game plan was to move forward and push the Germans back. When they landed, his sergeant would always inspect his plane for damage. Although Rogers came close to getting shot down many times, his planes were always taking the bullets for him. He was very lucky that none of his planes went down. They'd fly with almost no protection, unarmed. "We were not flying with any protective equipment at all," he said. "We flew with those leather helmets on and basically the cloth uniforms we were wearing. They wanted us to carry a .45 pistol with us. It was very heavy, so we stopped carrying those. And no parachutes."

Rogers remembered he had logged 120 missions. Although he was flying every day, he still had some blocks of time off. At first, he flew a couple of months nonstop. They then decided to give him some R&R. He stayed in the city of Grenoble in southern France. "At first, I didn't know why, but then I knew." (He demonstrated his hands shaking.) "You had to get a certain amount of tenseness, I suppose." He remembered driving up the hills and skiing on his days off. He didn't get another break for many months after that; by then, it was a much-needed relief.

As for news and keeping track of the other parts of the war, Rogers replied like most of the rest. "I wasn't sure at the time. I just tried to do my best." Everything was handled one day at a time. There was no way of knowing what else was going on in the world.

Chapter 4

On Being Lucky, Very Lucky

When Rogers didn't have a specific mission, they'd go searching for "targets of opportunity"—areas that needed reporting to fire at or just to be marked on charts. One such mission stood out in Rogers's mind. "We were in the Forty-Fourth Infantry Division in the Seventh Army, on the left side of the Seventh; on the right side of the Third was [General] Patton. For some reason, we kept looking for targets well behind the German lines." Rogers went on without missing a beat. "We would do that every once in a while, looking for targets. All of a sudden, we came across this hell of a great tank battle at a little village, a crossroads type of thing. Each side was shooting the devil out of each other, firing those tanks something terrible. We were up there, me and my observer ... His name was Kelley, and he was from Oklahoma City. So we were watching the battle down there. We hadn't been there very long, of course, and all of a sudden there were streams of red tracer bullets, probably .50-caliber bullets that came up and almost went through our right wing. It was instant. I pushed the plane over to go down and turn to go back, and when I did, there was Kelley saying, 'Let's get out of here!'"

Upon returning, they were notified by the sergeant of a hole about a foot behind where Kelley was, as well as many other holes in the aircraft. A bullet had also gone into the left rudder pedal, missing Rogers's left foot only by inches. "So the plane was pretty well riddled with bullet holes. Every time you went up, you were going to get some bullet holes."

When they crossed the Rhine, it was right between Worms and Mannheim, two large German cities close together. "We were up at about three thousand feet that time. There were an awful lot of ack-ack and things going on. All of a sudden, they started shooting the German 88 [millimeter gun] that was breaking [bursting in the air], and there were clusters of four that would break. They were close, they were really close. So once again, I put it into a turn and a steep dive. The plane was redlined at 120 and I was going 140 miles an hour with full throttle straight down. Before I got down, I headed for a huge cloud … Must have been an oil refinery that was hit and blown up and on fire. It had a huge black cloud, so I flew to hide behind that cloud. Before I got down, they fired two more volleys that broke around me. What was very interesting [is that] after the war, one of my friends told me [that] after he crossed the Rhine, he saw that too. He had seen the Germans trying to hit me."

He ended up flying in the Alps. Even the German Luftwaffe wouldn't let their small aircraft fly in the Alps. "And with good reason," said Rogers. "The winds are tremendous. If they're coming from one side, you'll go up like an elevator. And if they are coming from the other side, in a [Piper] Cub, even with all your power, you're still gonna go down."

They chased some Germans into Innbrooks, Austria. "There was a blizzard on the outside of the Alps. When we came out, we were flying in the blizzard, not what you want to be flying in. It's not a good idea to stay up, so I spotted a house near a field to land in. We went in and told them we were going to stay all night with them. They were German civilians—they always let you. We stayed. They didn't give us any food though. It got dark and I kept going out to check on the weather. I said to the observer, 'C'mon, let's go.' We went out with our fingers and scraped the wings off [of ice and snow], the elevators and rudder and everything. So we took off and flew back. They picked out a new landing field because of them moving. There were hundred-foot pine trees all around it and power lines in the middle. By the time we got there, it was pitch-black, nine o'clock at night.

"The value of the little Cub, it won't stall. The Cub will mush, so I put it in a mush-stall, just enough power so it's going [down] mush, mush, mush. After I went down the last pine tree, I went down like an elevator. I was mushing down and forward. When you land, you always look out [your cockpit] forty-five degrees. You never look out your front 'cause you can't tell anything. You look out forty-five [degrees] and there's snow all over the ground. When I saw we were going to land, I saw we were nose high and I wanted to be nose high. I wanted the tail wheel to hit first. I didn't know when that was going to happen, so I went and we got down there. I waited until the tail wheel hit the ground; then the nose went down. I gave it a lot of gas and the propeller took us down. I tied down the plane with the others and walked to the headquarters building.

"When we got in, the major asked, 'Where'd you come from?' I told him we flew in. He said, 'You couldn't have. We have a hard time landing in the daytime.' The major said to one of the other pilots, 'Go out and see if his plane is out there.' He came back and said, 'Yes sir, it's out there.' The major said, 'I don't know how you did it.' It was risky, but luckily, that little Cub saved me."

Rogers's stories were beginning to flow now. "One time, when I was taking off, I happened to look up and saw a German jet. That was a first, a German jet. I didn't even know they had a jet. It was silver, and I saw him, and he started to turn to come down on me, so luckily I put the plane down quick. I was only about fifty feet up in the air. I had just taken off and saw some big woods, so I just kept it between the woods and me. But the major in charge of headquarters battery said I saved his life, because he saw me do that and he was coming down the road in a jeep. He told the driver to pull right over. They pulled over and hopped out of the jeep. The jet came down and strafed the whole road, hitting the jeep and everything."

During his time moving the Third Reich into a retreat, he flew over the Danube River through Bavaria. Rogers flew into the Alps through the Inn Valley—with the highest peak being 13,284 feet—expecting some more of both dangerous winds and enemy fire. Rogers, as was his job, was heading right where the Germans were going. The town was Landeck, where a unit of the German Wehrmacht, the unified forces of Nazi Germany's army, navy, and air force, were camped out.

Rogers found his little Cub between German fire and the leeward winds descending on him. Once again, he gave the little plane full power—only to have it descend as the ferocious mountain winds pushed the Cub toward the German gunnery. And once again, Rogers didn't know if he'd make it. He was able to finally gain control of the aircraft to climb. "We went back just over the trees, ice and snow," he said—to avert yet another eminent disaster.

"One of these pilots, who was supposed to be one of the best pilots, named Martin, he came to me and said, 'Charlie, I've been taking this major up and he wants to get an air medal if he gets enough time in.' He said, 'I understand you have the dawn patrol?' I said I did. He said, 'I want to trade with you.' So he went on the dawn patrol and there were two Messerschmitts waiting for him. One of them, the low one, came in and riddled the plane with bullets. The major was killed, and the pilot wasn't killed but had holes all over him. So he was gone for the rest of the war. I was lucky there. He crash-landed, and a German farmer was nice enough to take him to a local hospital."

On VE (Victory in Europe) Day, Rogers was flying in the Alps down through the valley. They'd turn right toward the town of Fussen, Germany. As he turned right, he ran into a tremendous downstream of air from the mountains and started to descend rapidly. "I was probably about fifteen hundred feet up," he said. He couldn't change directions or altitudes, and it was a narrow valley. Sweating it out, he didn't know if he could outlast the turbulent air long enough to climb back up or find a field to land in. Once over the little town of Fussen, he knew the Germans occupied it. "I had to turn around at about maximum, six hundred feet, turn around in a very short amount of time ... expecting gunfire that entire time. They could have fired small arms, anything, but never a shot. What I found out when I got back was that that was the day the armistice was being signed in that section. So that saved me that day. The Germans would have made mincemeat out of me if they were still fighting. I thank the Lord every day."

Another tough flight had Rogers flying in a drenching rain. He had to go up and relay an important message to another troop. The pouring rain was so thick, Rogers was unable to see out his windscreen. Crabbing the plane into the wind with the nose high into the air—with his window open and his head out the side to see through the rain—Rogers made the dangerous flight successful. His luck had continued.

Soon after Germany's Third Reich had surrendered, Rogers and his troops were in the south of Munich. He saw a notice on a bulletin board offering pilots the opportunity to switch over and fly for the Third Corps. Rogers was still upset with his major because he'd been passed over for the rank of first lieutenant, which had been promised him upon reaching England. He took the change to the Third and went to the outskirts of Innsbruck, Austria. Once again, he was flying a Stinson aircraft, which was quite a bit faster and much bigger than his little Cub. The army used these planes for courier service, taking generals and high-ranking officials from and to Munich and Nancy, France.

On another "lucky flight," Rogers went from Innsbruck to Nancy, flying a Stinson aircraft. A German mechanic had worked on it and gotten it ready for him. Apparently that was not uncommon at the time; once Germany surrendered, many non-Nazis helped the Allies. When he landed in France, he asked them to top off his fuel tanks. The man filling the tanks told him he had run out of gas just when he'd landed. Rogers had had a bad feeling about that German mechanic and wondered if he had intentionally neglected to fill the tanks when he left.

Rogers did get to fly a German aircraft, a low-wing predecessor of the Messerschmitt. "They used it as a trainer," he said. "It would go between 150 and 200 miles an hour. That was a fast little plane, tiny little tires. They would put down temporary [aircraft] fields made of steel links hooking together. To get one of those devils off the ground, you had to get it off on one wheel first, then yank it off." One time, the winds had changed 180 degrees and the buildings were close to the end of the runway. He took off on one wheel and yanked the stick back hard to begin his climb, but it didn't look like he was going to clear one of the buildings. He pulled one wing up on a steep bank and it barely made its way over the building as he slowly climbed, watching his wingtips clear. He really sweated that one out.

Rogers also flew a German Bucker, a maneuverable aerobatic biplane the Germans used to harass the Allies. Another one of his lucky flights found him coming back from Nancy, France, above a thick cloud layer. He was getting very worried that he wasn't seeing any openings or holes below him. He was additionally worried about the hills and mountaintops he knew were just below those clean white layers—as well as his limited fuel capacity. He eventually found a small hole and nosed the Bucker down through the hole beneath the cloud layer and in sight of land again. Flying on top with limited fuel can be terrifying, especially knowing the mountainous terrain is waiting for your mistakes.

Chapter 5

Enough Already?

ARE WE REALLY HEADING TO JAPAN FROM HERE?

When the war in Europe ended, Roger's commanding officer of the Forty-Fourth Infantry Division, General William F. Dean Sr., went to the supreme commanding officer, General Dwight D. Eisenhower, and offered to have his troops participate in the Japan invasion. (General Dean went on to fight in the Korean War. Unfortunately, he was famous for being the highest-ranking officer to be captured.)

Rogers was part of the first full division out of Germany. He returned to New York on the *Queen Mary*. Celebrations were in full swing. Marlene Dietrich and families and friends of all the soldiers on board greeted them at the dock. "There was a hell of a lot of noise going on," recalled Rogers. "Horns were blowing. It was marvelous."

After a week's leave, Rogers was on to another training camp in Arkansas to learn how to invade Japan. That war was still raging, with the Japanese vowing to fight till the last man's last breath.

The new methods of launching planes (which Rogers was learning) were very scary. There was a hundred-yard cable with an arm that came down and connected to a wirelike merry-go-round. The aircraft were hooked to it by the top of the plane. As the pilot added full power (while being connected), he waved his hand when ready and they'd cut him loose to fly—one after the other. The landings were similar—by catching the top of the aircraft to the cable hook.

Fortunately for Rogers and the rest of the country, the Japanese totally surrendered on August 15, 1945, and signed the instrument of surrender on September 2, 1945. As we all know, it took two atomic bombs being detonated over Japan for the surrender to occur. The first one was over Hiroshima on August 6, 1945, and the second was over Nagasaki on August 9, 1945, which forced the Imperial Japanese Army to completely surrender to the Allies. At the time, Rogers, like many other Americans, felt no pity for the Japanese upon hearing that this new bomb had been dropped. "It was the right thing to do to save lives on both sides. It was the right thing to do to end the war," Rogers said.

HONORABLE DISCHARGE

Charles F. Rogers was honorably discharged from US Army Air Force in July 1945 at Fort Dix, New Jersey. In addition to his World War II ribbons, Rogers was awarded an Air Medal with two Oak Leaf Clusters for his service. Rogers came home as a first lieutenant. If he had stayed in longer, he would have been promoted to captain. He didn't want his good luck to run out. He'd had many close calls and difficult flights.

Charlie and Mary were married for sixty-nine years. They had five children. Their oldest, a daughter, predeceased them. The Rogers had an additional four boys: Charles "Chuck," Brian (an artist like his dad), Jay, and finally the baby, Jonathan. As of this writing, Rogers has seven grandchildren and three great-grandchildren.

When asked about flying after he returned, Rogers replied, "I flew a little after the war. I didn't care about just flying around. I wanted to fly for a living, but they were flying for hire in Egypt. I wasn't interested. I also wanted to get back into my artwork."

After the war, he once took his wife, Mary, for a flight over his family's house. They were doing turns around the house while waving at those below; his sister was out there, waving back up at them with their black Scottie dog barking like something from an old black-and-white movie. Mary wasn't too keen on flying and didn't enjoy Rogers's ability to perform steep turns and climbs and fast dives—that one flight was enough for her.

Upon returning and settling down, Rogers fulfilled his childhood dream and went into business for himself as an art director for several large companies. He ventured out successfully in many other avenues as well, including a nationwide mail order business.

Rogers was the president of the Mail Orders Association, which boasted 3,400 members throughout the country. During one period, he worked for a company called Stern's Nurseries, the inventors of Miracle-Gro. Rogers helped design and sell the amazing product in its infancy years. He eventually retired in 1986.

For twenty-three years after retirement, the Rogerses avoided the harsh New England winters and headed for the sunny skies of Florida. I'm convinced Rogers would have made one heck of a flight instructor, but he had pushed his luck more than a clowder of cats.

Your luck and courage paved the way for your future and the future of all Americans. Thank you, Charlie Rogers for all you sacrificed.

ROGERS WITH HIS TRUSTED PIPER CUB.

"GRASSHOPPER PILOT."

PIPER CUB SIMILAR TO THE ONE ROGERS FLEW
JUST BARELY OVER THE TREETOPS.

Book 10

Staff Sergeant
Lauri K. Rautio

Chapter 1

Some of the Bad Memories
I Just Stuffed Away

Lauri K. Rautio was born in Fitchburg, Massachusetts, on May 12, 1925. Lauri's parents, Nata and Amanda Rautio, were both born in Finland. They made their way to the United States around 1912, but not together, because they hadn't yet met. They both ended up in Fitchburg after arriving via Boston. His mom was just a single young girl traveling alone; she didn't speak English yet. Somehow, she managed to board the correct train to Fitchburg, and met up with other relatives and Finnish people there. The Saima Society was a large social organization that helped Finnish people in Fitchburg adapt to American ways. Saima hosted many events for the large Finnish population. Lauri's parents met as a result of one of those meetings. Nata and Amanda had two boys who would make their parents extremely proud in the years to come.

Lauri's older brother, Unto, was born on January 20, 1919. The elder was a big influence on his younger brother. The older Rautio was an avid small-aircraft builder when they were young. Lauri remembered how his brother would build and fly his model airplanes. Both boys were real "airplane buffs," loving anything aviation. Like many US citizens after the Pearl Harbor invasion, Unto joined the United States Army Air Force, enlisting on January 12, 1942. He went to school to become an aircraft engine mechanic and eventually became a crew-chief mechanic for US fighter planes. He was assigned to the Eighth Army, 487th Fighter Squadron, 352nd Fighter Group. Unto's group was stationed in Bodney, England, and became known as the Bastards from Bodney. Unto was a mechanic for two flying aces, also from the 487th: Captain William "Bill" Whisner and First Lieutenant Al Rigby.

Unto saw a lot of military action and worked hard to keep the P-51 Mustangs flying. As a result, he was awarded an Air Medal and a Bronze Star for his efforts. Talking with Lauri, it was clear that his older brother was his real hero.

Lauri Rautio was a lower–ball turret gunner in a B-17. He was in the mighty Eighth Army Air Corps, 447th Bomb Group (Heavy) and the 708th Squadron. At nineteen years old, he started his missions of flying in B-17s at Rattlesden, England. His first mission was flown on Christmas Eve 1944, and his last mission—number twenty-three— occurred on April 16, 1945.

"In my midteens, the government started a program to train us young folks to fill a void people needed for the war effort," Lauri said. "I entered an NYA [National Youth Administration] program for aircraft mechanics and was sent to school at Quoddy Village in Maine. Food, housing, and ten dollars a month for personal effects and free schooling on the current day's aircraft engines—I loved it! Upon completion of the school, I was offered a job as an aircraft engines assistant mechanic at Rome, New York, Army Air Corps base. While mulling over this offer, an article in our local newspaper appeared, indicating there was to be exams given locally for entrance into the Air Corps Air Cadets program for pilot, navigator, and bombardier candidates. I promptly signed up to take these exams. Out of approximately one hundred young men taking these exams, about twenty passed. I was one of them. Shortly thereafter, I volunteered for induction, as I felt I would probably soon be drafted anyway. This way I'd be more apt to enter the branch of service I really preferred."

Rautio was shipped to basic training for aviation cadets at Keesler Field in Biloxi, Mississippi, for a twelve-week program. He was then sent to another twelve-week program at the University of Alabama for more intensive training, including twelve hours of Piper J-3 Cub flight training. However, the war effort had other plans for him. He received orders one week before completion of this program that he was "Eliminated [from this program] without prejudice for the convenience of the U.S. Government." He was a week away from attending the desirable primary flight school training. He was already classified for pilot training, his "fondest wish," but Rautio would now be attending a gunnery school in Kingman, Arizona. He'd still be in the air flying, but as a gunner instead of a pilot. Always a pilot at heart, he breezed through the aircraft recognition section of training—as well as gunnery school, which included assembling, disassembling, maintaining, and operating the .50-caliber guns he'd be using on the aircraft he'd be flying in.

They'd practice shooting shotguns at clay pigeons from the back of a moving truck. From there, it was on to air-to-air and air-to-ground practice, with further training in aircraft turrets until it was all second nature. Upon graduating, Rautio received his wings and was off to Drew Field in Tampa, Florida, to meet his crew—ten men who would be serving together as long as possible in a B-17 heavy bomber. Rautio's assignment was a "ball turret gunner and armorer." He was joined by First Lieutenant Pilot Alvin D. Mayhew, Second Lieutenant Copilot Edward P. Lukomski, Second Lieutenant Carl A. Dossenbach, Tech Sergeant Frank E. Kravetz, Second Lieutenant Abraham M. Haddad, Second Lieutenant Donald J. Funk, Tech Sergeant Alfred E. Dusey, and Staff Sergeant Lloyd W. Hickman.

At first, the crew appeared that it would have troubles; the navigator assigned to his crew had already gone down once in the swamps of Florida. Rautio remembered vividly one training exercise when they almost exploded on takeoff. He was manning the right waist window and looking outside as the large aircraft ascended. He saw fuel pouring out over the wing as though it were being flushed from a fire hose. The fuel was vaporizing as it ran past the trailing edge of the wing; it also appeared that there were small sparks coming from beneath the wing. "If the two would have met, we would have turned into a rocket immediately," said Rautio. A quick intercom call and the pilot shut down that engine, feathered the prop, banked left, and immediately landed. The fuel cap on the third engine had come off and fuel was being suctioned out, a small mistake that could have proven disastrous. Luck and courage would be a part of Rautio's everyday life from now on.

Chapter 2

We Were Going to War!

U pon completion of his Replacement Training Unit in Florida, their orders came in to deploy to the European theater of operations. Rautio and his crew were shipped to Manchester, New Hampshire, to pick up a new B-17G model aircraft for their flight to Valley, Wales, in the United Kingdom. The ferry ride over wasn't all that uneventful either. The first leg of the trip included a stop in Goose Bay, Labrador. Rautio was given guard duty of the ship. He recalled, "It was bitterly cold. The aircraft fuselage kept out most of the wind. I had a military arctic sleeping bag, which I laid out on the radio room floor. Climbing into the sleeping bag fully clothed, I found this down-filled bag surprisingly warm. After some time, I had to climb out and remove my shoes and flight jacket before getting back into the sack. Somewhat later, I repeated this process, removing my wool trousers. Finally, comfy in my bag and tired from the day's events, I fell asleep … on guard duty."

Rautio was soon awakened by the sound and shaking of an engine roaring on this giant bomber during his watch. "I bounded out of my sleeping bag, my .45 pistol in hand, and virtually ran through the bomb bay up to the cockpit area, where there was a GI sitting in the pilot's seat manipulating the engine controls. I challenged him with my pistol in his face and frightened the poor guy beyond description. He kept repeating, 'I'm a mechanic—supposed to check out that engine!' I had not been advised of someone coming out. Standing there, mostly disrobed, I was beginning to freeze, so I decided to accept the situation and rushed back to my sleeping bag. The night passed and I stayed awake ... a better soldier.

"We remained in Goose Bay for several days, awaiting proper weather before departing for Keflavic, Iceland." Although the flight over the North Atlantic was uneventful, Rautio remembered seeing icebergs and what looked like very cold water. Upon finally landing at Valley, Rautio had several different assignments, but he remembered one in particular: being assigned guard duty of GI luggage and given a Thompson submachine gun. He was "standing guard in a sentry box at night. It was so-so black dark," he recalled. "We were in a country at war for some time now. Everything was blacked out—absolutely *no* light allowed to be emitted from anywhere. I stood in that sentry box listening for any sounds. I heard some kind of sound and moved quietly out of the box, which was placed next to a fence. I could not see anything, but I could sense something huge in the darkness not far from me. I hand charged the submachine gun and shouted, 'WHO GOES THERE?' Instantly there was a snort, and the figure ran off into the darkness. I had narrowly fired on a horse corralled in the fenced area behind me! It was a little hairy for a young soldier in a new environment."

Chapter 3

With a Christmas Eve
Never Forgotten

R autio and his crew found themselves in a railcar headed for their base near Stowmarket, England, named Rattlesden. The men were assigned a Quonset hut as their new home. Up to two dozen men shared this hut from various crews. Simple daily living and chores were difficult, supplies were limited, and there were rules and guards to police those rules. Inside the hut was a cast-iron potbellied stove. This was intended to keep them warm, along with about a wheelbarrow of soft coal per week. The airmen worked out the "guard schedule," so one man from their hut was always on watch for the base's coal allotments. As a result, they enjoyed at least double their regular allotment for a while.

Their Yankee ingenuity continued beyond a basic coal stove. Once again, the clever airmen worked together to adapt their coal stove so it would burn old oil mixed with aviation fuel, which was 110-octane leaded gas. They used an old oxygen tank (from a wrecked B-17) as an oil storage tank, connected to aircraft hydraulic lines (smuggled from aircraft wrecks) through the hut wall and into the lower base of the stove. Concoct a shut-off valve/regulator, ignite the fuel in the stove, and PRESTO—heat.

Uniforms also needed to be cleaned and presentable. The crews found a solution. They'd "dry clean" them by drenching the uniforms in a bucket of avgas and simply hang them on the barbed-wire fence behind their hut long enough to dry. "The fuel was so volatile that the fresh air would completely evaporate the fuel and not leave even a smell. You just had to make sure it was left out long enough," added Rautio.

Another issue needing to be overcome in this new environment was general clothes washing. The officers had arrangements with civilians outside the base. "We enlisted personnel had to work around that problem," Rautio said. Once again, the crew found a solution. One of the guys found a large steel half-shaped sphere container. They built a stone footing under the sphere, large enough to build a fire under it. They made a cover from scrap wood and a paddle. And a washing machine was born. "Put water and soap in, build a fire underneath it, throw clothing in and several guys take turns agitating the contents. It worked great."

On Christmas Eve 1944, Rautio and his crew flew their first combat mission. The mission was to Zellhausen, Germany, and the flight lasted nine long hours. Rautio remembered that first one in great detail. "I would enter my ball turret at approximately 'coast in' to the European continent, after crossing the English Channel, and back out roughly the same point on return. That meant I was in my turret perhaps five to six hours. I had never previously been in that turret over perhaps one and a half hours continuously during training. There was a point during that first mission when every nerve in my body was screaming to get the hell out of that turret. Of course, that was not possible. It was my duty to stay and cover the underbelly of the aircraft. After a period of time, this urge to get out of the turret passed, and I became reasonably comfortable there. I never again had that urge to exit my turret."

Rautio explained, "The ball turret was a thirty-six-inch-diameter sphere with a clamshell door, which served as my back rest. There were two latches in my shoulder area to hold this door closed. There was a safety belt, which passed across the door area back of my neck. In the turret were two .50-caliber Browning machine guns, one on either side of me. These guns had about 1,175 rounds of ammunition. The gun sight was positioned in front of my face. Two handles were on either side of the gun sight to operate the turret. The handles were twisted left, right, up, or down to rotate the turret. The more twist, the more rapidly the turret would rotate. Buttons on the ends of the handles would operate the guns. One foot operated the gun sight reticles, which were set to the enemy aircraft wingspan." Rautio continued, "Also in the turret was the attach points for the oxygen supply for my mask, the plug for my electrically heated suit, and the intercom system." In the turret, there was also a chute to dump out his empty shell casings. Rautio refrained from just dumping them until he knew none of his other bombers were below him.

Usually, most ball turret gunners flew without their parachute being readily available. On a few missions, Rautio squeezed his chest-pack chute in with him. He entered the turret, clipped only one side of the chute to his harness, and swung it around like an armrest. He devised a quick solution, if needed. "I'd unlatch the turret door and the safety belt in back of my neck, fasten the clips to my harness, clip the chute to the harness, then quickly pull out the plugs for the oxygen, suit heat, and intercom, and push out of the turret to fall free."

Rautio explained the process for entering the ball turret in detail. "The turret had a clutch, which engaged its operating mechanism to either manual or power. It was necessary to hand crank the turret so the guns were pointed straight down, and then the clamshell door could be opened. I could then step down into the turret, stepping on the small seat, a small piece of armor plate. Then I would hook up the oxygen line to my mask, plug in my heated flying suit, worn under my flying suit. The jacket had the pants plugged into them, and in turn the 'slippers' plugged into the pants. On the sleeves, the gloves plugged in, then attach the intercom system."

Like the others, Rautio described the flying weather over the United Kingdom as "mostly absolutely horrible." The fog was thick and dangerous. Aircraft by the hundreds would be taking off in near zero visibility to join the combat formations. He recalls that "southeast England was like one big aircraft carrier." On many occasions, Rautio, standing at the waist gunner's position as they climbed through the fog, witnessed a bright giant flash through the clouds and knew it was the "impact of a couple heavy bombers loaded with fuel and tons of high explosives as well as ammunition" colliding in the fog.

Another common killer for airmen was anoxia, the absence of oxygen. Climbing beyond twelve thousand feet required the crew to don oxygen masks, and the temperatures at their altitudes of over twenty-five thousand feet would be around minus 60 degrees Fahrenheit. Moisture from breathing would oftentimes freeze and cause malfunctions on the mask. Without any warning, one would pass out within minutes. "Our navigator served as our safety officer," Rautio said. "He'd call out on the intercom every few minutes for an oxygen check. The entire crew, from the tail to the nose, would respond in turn. The nearest crewman immediately checked anyone 'missing' in response. Our flight engineer/ top turret gunner and myself were once pulled from our position and fed more oxygen after turning blue in color."

Chapter 4

Missions from My Wartime Diary

Following are accounts of some of Rautio's missions taken directly from his handwritten diary. In between the bad, he'd find some good. All are amazing stories and are edited only for style and clarity:

I remember sitting in my turret on one mission, just rotating the turret. Up, down, around, just searching, in my own thoughts, alone, just the drone of the engines and the slipstream whisking around the turret and the intercom quiet, and in my mind, I thought I could hear the angels singing. It was distant and like a church choir. Eerie indeed! But sort of peaceful at the same time. The thought passed in my head, *I wonder if this is going to be 'my day'?* It was not at all upsetting though.

December 24, Christmas Eve 1944. Mission 1: [He was with his crew in the *Ole Boomerang*, and the target was into Zellhausen, Germany. They flew for nine hours at 22,700 feet. The temperature was minus 36 Celsius.] My ball turret Plexiglas was sprayed with water on takeoff. As a result, when it froze, visibility was completely cut off through the sighting window. When I test fired the right gun, it fired several rounds and stopped. After a couple hours, hydraulic fluid began to spray out on me from the Vickers unit. [They were able to easily hit their target with no flak inbound. However, on returning, one ship blew up and went down in flames in front of them.] A direct hit in the left wing. No chutes were seen to come out.

December 31, 1944. Mission 3, heading to Hamburg Germany.

More luck than courage got them home safely. They were assigned one of six aircraft with no bomb load, to fly ahead of the group. The purpose was to drop chaff strips that would interrupt the enemy radar for the bombers. "The flak was very intense and accurate," recalled Rautio. He was able to shoot both guns through his half-frozen turret accurately. Three of the six ships were blown up. They were hit with thirteen flak holes. Their fuel was very low, and they were all sweating this one out. "One of the crew had become hysterical and needed some help. Heavy smoke and fire were everywhere." The flight was eight hours, mostly over the North Sea.

January 1, 1945. Mission 4: Daulenberg, Germany. [*Ole Boomerang* was leaving in thick, dense fog once again. As a result, one ship crashed on takeoff with a full bomb load. As always, their targets were very specific and exact. Today's was oil storage tanks near Brunswick. They were chased by ME262 German jets.] [The crew member] went haywire again today, this is getting serious. He was on intercom and in fear, holding the button down and that blocks the radio, talking about airplanes up at nine o'clock high. They were B-17 squadrons flying with us. His airplane recognition is bad.

January 6, 1945. Mission 7: Target was Worms, Germany. Today's mission was to knock out some of Germany's transportation. Our load consisted of ten 500-lb g.p. bombs and two 500-lb incendiary bomb clusters. We took off in horrible weather again this morning. The weather ship ahead of us crashed and burned on takeoff. The ammunition was blowing off in all directions as the fire consumed the aircraft. Fortunately, there were no bombs on the ship and no one on the ground was injured. The temperatures were freezing on the ground so that made everything more difficult. We bombed by instruments through an overcast. The group on our left dropped on a target before we got to ours and theirs was visual. I tracked their bombs down and seen them hit right in a large town. A few seconds later, fires blinked everywhere down there. In a short time the place was an inferno and soon the smoke blotted out the scene. The mission lasted almost eight hours. Today he didn't fly with us. We had a replacement waist gunner.

January 7, 1945. Mission 8: Hamm, Germany: The Luftwaffe was expected up today—and they were. ... We had an escort of seven full groups of P-51s—sweet boys. Enemy fighters were up today but we weren't hit. They followed the other two divisions back to England but the peashooters kept them off.

January 14, 1945. Mission 9: Magdeburg, Germany. Another "cooks tour" is what we found out was in store for us when we walked into briefing at about 3:00 this morning. Today's target, we were told, if hit well, would eliminate 16 percent of Germany's vital oil reserve. We were briefed for 70 heavy (88s and 155s) guns at the target. Everything was quiet, as always. We flew up around the North Sea area, by Helgoland, through Stettin past a flak area between Berlin and Brandenburg. We got flak on the way into enemy territory over Stettin. I saw one B-17 blow up and go down flaming, disintegrating all the way down and then blow up when it hit the ground again. Boy, that's a hell of a feeling, sitting there waiting, but no chutes came out.

At the target on the bomb run the Gerries were using a barrage, a terrific barrage. I seen the squadron ahead of us "get it." One second the sky would be just bare, then the next, right in the squadron, it would be filled with bursting flak. Then we came through—and no flak! Then the squadron behind us came through and the same barrage. It was so intense I couldn't see how they ever bored through like they did. We figured later that we must have caught them just as they were reloading.

That mission had other issues other than flak. During oxygen check, one of the gunners, Dusey, didn't respond. Ed, the copilot, got to him just in time. His mask had become frozen and he was blue. Ed put the ox on him 100 percent and Dusey came back. There were also plenty of dogfights between the Luftwaffe and the P-51's "peashooters." The Luftwaffe were taking a beating from our fighters, blowing them up as they came close and also on the ground before they could even depart to come after us. Another eight-hour flight.

January 20, 1945. Mission 11: Aulendorf, Germany.
[Today they went out to "hammer at the railways of
Germany." They were hit "only about four times" today.]
We spent an extra hour over the target thus wasting a
lot of fuel, so on the way back, we were forced down at
Merville, France. It's really hard to write my impressions
when we first landed or seen the field.

As they were on final approach, Rautio noticed a B-24 nosed into
the ground, tail sticking up in the air. While taxiing, the surrounding
area was littered with destroyed B-17s, B-24s, and P-51s that had all
crash-landed.

The crew was given some time off and went into town, which had
been in German hands just a couple of weeks earlier. Rautio described
the town as in "shambles"—destroyed, shot up, riddled with bullet
holes everywhere. To make matters worse, Rautio recalled, "The feeling
towards Americans was not as high as would be expected."

February 3, 1945. Mission 13: Berlin, Germany. I
never felt as sick, or to be truthful, had such a scared
feeling deep in my stomach before a mission as I did
this morning, when the screen in front of the map was
rolled up in the briefing room and I saw the mission,
"the Big B." The mission was in support of the Russian
Army in their offensive against Berlin. The target was
communications in the heart of the capitol. To be exact,
our target was Wilhemstrasse. While taxiing out to the
runway, the aircraft blew a tire. The crew sighed with
relief, hoping they wouldn't have to make the perilous
journey. However, the ground crew had it changed and
ready to fly in 20 minutes.

We bombed from an altitude of 25,500 feet, temperature was minus 45 C. Flak over the target really amazed us as we expected it to be much heavier. It was moderate and quite inaccurate. We were in enemy territory for four hours, in the air for nine hours and fifteen minutes, on oxygen for six hours. Our load was twelve 500-lb. bombs. Mixed incendiary clusters, demolitions, and delayed action demolition bombs. Some delayed as much as a full week!

We had an escort of five groups of P-51s. We got no battle damage. It really looked like a parade over there today. Definite proof of Allied air superiority. As far as the eye could see to the front and rear were groups of B-17 Forts and mixed all over in groups of about four above, below and to the sides—P-51s. All those planes roaming over Germany as they pleased, unmolested by enemy aircraft. After we had flown several hundred miles we could still look back and see where Berlin was by the clouds of smoke coming high above the clouds. It's a sight one can never forget.

March 14, 1945. Mission 14: Hanover, Germany.

After a period of five weeks of not flying, the crew was at it again. After the thirteenth mission, *Ole Bomerang* was reconfigured as a pathfinder. "On a pathfinder aircraft, the ball turret was removed and a radar dome was mounted in its position," Rautio said. "I now was moved into the waist [gunner's] position and the previous waist gunner went to some other crew."

March 18, 1945. Mission 15: Berlin, Germany. Today, we were part of the biggest daytime air raid of Berlin since the war had started. Over 1,800 heavy bombers from the Mighty Eighth Air Force rained 3,000 tons of high explosive on the Nazi capital.

March 30, 1945. Mission 18: Hamburg, Germany. Things now were getting desperate for the Nazi war effort, however, their ME 262 jets were now buzzing them like bees. Both fighters and bombers were firing at each other from distances closer than 1,000 yards. There was plenty of flak holes throughout the aircraft. Including one right through the bomb bay door that was actually stopped by a bomb! On the way back over the North Sea, (engine) numbers 3 and 4 cut out and began windmilling. They were beginning to lose altitude quite fast as the B-17 weighed in around 65,000 lbs. Fortunately, the issue was simply a fuel transfer valve. It needed to be manually activated and the Flight Engineer was unfamiliar with this procedure of this aircraft.

April 8, 1945. Mission 20: Plauen, Germany. [Things were about to look seriously bad for *Ole Boomerang*, her crew, and the others.] I was standing in my position, looking out the window at our wingman on the right side, when suddenly the aircraft [I was watching] was hit by a burst of flak on the left horizontal stabilizer/elevator, blowing it completely off! At the moment of impact the tail gunner was hunched down. It appeared he was doing something with his guns, perhaps hand charging them. He sat bolt upright immediately and looked out to see the stabilizer was completely gone! His head swiveled left, right, here and there trying to assimilate what had happened. The tail appeared to drop slightly lower and the pilot moved [the aircraft] slightly out and away from us, the lead aircraft, as the [hit aircraft] pilot stabilized his flight attitude flying a mild "S" pattern outward and inward beside us. The left stabilizer unit had been blown off so clean the airplane continued to fly very well. The vertical stabilizer and rudder were perforated completely with flak holes. But somehow, miraculously, the tail gunner appeared to be none the worse, not hit. The [gunner], observing that they continued flying with the rest of the squadron as before, just sat back in his position and continued his ride. This Sergeant I later learned was from Texas, and his pilot, Lt. Mustaleski (a Midwesterner), continued with us over the target, dropped their bombs and returned home to Rattlesden. I believe the pilot earned a Distinguished Flying Cross for that bit of flying. And the wonderful Boeing B-17 earned more love and respect from the rest of us.

In the fuselage, there were two 'relief tubes,' one up front and another in the rear section. These were, as the name implies, for the crew members to relieve their bladders when necessary. The temperature at altitudes were on average 50–60 degrees below zero. When someone in the front of the airplane had to relieve himself, the relief tube drew the contents into the slipstream, which blew back onto the glass on the front of my turret, and instantly froze! Forward visibility through the gun sight was totally impaired for the entire mission. It was part of our learning curve. NO ONE forward of my turret in the airplane could relieve themselves without first advising me, so I could turn my turret straight aft (full facing rearward), thereafter.

April 8, 1945. Mission 20: Plauen, Germany. We flew at only 5,000 feet. This was the closest look I have yet had at German towns and some of our work—the results, that is. Some of those towns, big towns, had absolutely nothing left standing. Some, more fortunate, had a couple houses left and some "shells." The thing that struck me was, in one such town where everything was demolished, right in the center of the ruins standing untouched was the city's church. We saw two B-17s go down over a target just a few miles from ours. One blew up—the other went down a "flamer." Flak was intense.

April 9, 1945. Mission 21: Neunburg, Germany. Today's mission was the first time I've flown over enemy territory without even seeing flak.

Their target was a jet airfield close to the Czechoslovakian border. They could see the weaving trenches of the front line easily from that altitude. They could see the fires and smoke rising from the ongoing fighting of close troops below. The war wasn't over yet.

April 11, 1945. Mission 22: Ingolstadt, Germany. Again, today's target were the Luftwaffe airfields. But something was missing. On today's mission, we flew over and bombed German territory without any opposition of any kind. We saw no flak at all. Although fighter opposition was expected, we saw no enemy aircraft. We saw activity where the front lines are again—towns burning etc.

April 16, 1945. Mission 23: Le Verdo, France. Our last
bombing mission was over a German occupied area
of France. A section passed by during the previous
invasions, but one that was necessary to keep the push
forward. They were paving the way for Free French
ground troops, as was their mission.

Another mission had Rautio walking the catwalk to the bomb
doors to release a stuck five-hundred-pound bomb. They were over
Germany, and the pilot, Mayhew, called him over the intercom. "No
effort by the bombardier would toggle it out," Rautio said. "We could
most certainly *not* risk taking it home and landing with it on board, nor
could the bomb bay doors be closed." Rautio then explained the bombs
in great detail. "These bombs had two 'eyes' welded on the casings,
one toward the front, the other toward the tail. The fuses looked like
aluminum cans perhaps two inches in diameter and four to five inches
long. On one end of this can was a threaded … spring-loaded plunger,
which, when released, armed the bomb. This device had a propeller,
which would rotate a given number of turns when released [moved the
plunger] and arm the bomb. These propellers were kept from rotating
by a wire, which locked them from turning. The other end of that wire
was attached to the bomb racks. When dropped, the wire pulls out,
allowing the propeller to turn in the slipstream until it clears the aircraft
and pops off, arming the bomb.

"I could not wear the chest-pack parachute and perform the job to
be done. In the bomb bay was a walkway through the centerline to the
front cockpit area … about four or five inches wide. The bomb racks
were on each side of the walkway." To keep himself from falling through
the open doors while trying to release the bomb, Rautio had to unclip
the walkway divider ropes, pass them through his harness where the
chute would be, and reconnect them to the fuselage. "At the same time,
I had to safeguard my oxygen bailout bottle and a long screwdriver-like

tool I would need to try to release the hung-up bomb. It was windy and cold in there as I crossed the bomb bay to my job, and the view looking down into Germany, about five miles below through occasional flak bursts, was spectacular.

"I found the bomb was hung up by the tail-side hanger and it was tilted down about forty-five degrees. The safety wire for the nose fuse had pulled out when it had released, and the propeller on the nose of the five-hundred-pound bomb was rotating slowly. It hadn't yet popped the arming mechanism, as the wind was not as forceful as it would be after release. I tried to contain the propeller while I hung on to my oxygen bottle and jammed the tool into the eye of the hanger. After sufficient twisting and pounding and turning, the bomb dropped away free as the shackle opened. I made my way back aft and the bomb bay doors were closed."

Rautio has many stories, memories, and writings. He's truly an amazing American.

Chapter 5

Rautio Keeps on Flying Long after the Fires Burn Out

As the war was coming to a close, the Germans were getting hit hard at home in Berlin. The stretch of Allied aircraft was now thousands long. US bombers followed by the Royal Air Force seemed to fly nonstop. Rautio recalls the scene from his turret, "turning ninety degrees left to enter the city and again ninety degrees left after the bomb run to exit the city. As we flew on homeward, I remember looking back to Berlin. The clouds were lifting straight up, cliff-like, for thousands of feet above the city from the heat of the fires. It had to be hell on earth down there!"

Lauri Rautio spent 113 days overseas flying in B-17s, in which he flew an astonishing twenty-three grueling missions—every one surrounded by death and destruction, more in one average day than most of us will have to endure in many lifetimes. These brave men didn't make close friends; they were not sure they should believe in a tomorrow. They didn't even live one day at a time. They lived hour to hour, smiling whenever possible, kidding one another, and waiting for the next briefing.

Rautio was honorably discharged early; he had extra "points" that he'd accumulated from combat hours. Although the war wasn't over, it was close enough. The United States had reserves they were sending overseas, allowing Rautio to be released from his duties. He returned to Fitchburg and found work at the General Electric plant for a short time. He met Helen Tommila at a small Finnish restaurant. She was a waitress there, and Rautio would sit around and chat with her. The two were married in 1946. Rautio was at the bottom of the seniority list at GE and had received an offer to work as a draftsman at Great American Plastics. "Horrible mistake I made," Rautio said, still smirking about the move after all these years. He left GE for Great American Plastics. Unto was also a draftsman, and it didn't take much convincing on Lauri's part to get his big brother to work with him at Great American. The two worked together for a couple of years. Unto ended up at GE, and Lauri went to Simonds Saw and Steel. Lauri retired from Simonds after forty years of service with them in 1990.

Helen and Lauri had four children, three boys and one girl. The oldest son followed his dad's footsteps in the service as a paratrooper in Vietnam, retiring from the military after twenty years.

Throughout all his years, Rautio continued his love of aviation in many ways. He actually built his own aircraft from a set of plans, laboring on it for more than nine years. It was a single-seater aircraft, which he brought to the Fitchburg Airport in 1969 for its maiden flight. Rautio flew his first aircraft successfully for about eleven years. The two enjoyed many adventures together. Later he sold it to a friend in Canada but only after he had constructed a new one capable of carrying two passengers.

Several years later, in 2009, Rautio sold his second home-built aircraft as well. He felt his age was becoming a factor. However, he soon began constructing yet a third flying machine, which served until he finally decided to retire from flying at the age of eighty-nine. The third one, too, was finally sold and taken to Canada.

Thank you, Sergeant Lauri K. Rautio, for your twenty-three dangerous missions during those difficult years.

FROM THE COMBAT FLIGHT LOG OF:

S/SGT. LAURI K. RAUTIO 31389678
BALL TURRET GUNNER (MAYHEW CREW)
708 SQDN. 447ᵀᴴ BOMB GROUP (H)

AGE: 19 YRS.

RATTLESDEN, ENGLAND
1944

NINETEEN-YEAR OLD RAUTIO ALL GEARED UP AND READY.

MEMORIAL TO THE BRAVE 447ᵀᴴ BOMB
GROUP AT RATTLESDEN ENGLAND.

A VERY HONORABLE
MENTION

I n the process of writing this book, I personally interviewed two dozen or more veterans of World War II. They all had some very similar characteristics, the strongest one being the need to do their jobs to the best of their ability—knowing it all made a difference somehow, down to the smallest task. The enormous war machine's spokes were widespread; here are more stories of some of the other veterans I interviewed:

John F. Casey was born May 30, 1919. His parents were American born, and his grandparents were Irish immigrants. Casey came from a large family of thirteen children and had eleven sisters and one brother. He attended one year of high school and, as was so often the case, quit school to find work. On January 7, 1942, Casey was drafted into the US Army and in one of the first combat groups to go overseas. He remembered losing a few ships from bombings of their caravan on the way over the North Atlantic. "As far as you could see was ships," he said. They arrived in Liverpool, England.

Following are a few of Casey's stories after leaving England for France:

He couldn't swim and was terrified of the LSTs but had to use them like everyone else. "Everyone was scared. If they didn't say they were, they were lying." Casey clearly remembered being in an LST heading from England into France when a mine went off in front of them. He was inside, and the whole amphibious vehicle shook and shuddered. In that instant, he saw his entire family in his mind's eye—parents', sisters', and brothers' faces all flashed before him. He thought he was about to die and expected the great crash of water to overcome the LST and send them to the bottom of the sea.

They landed in Normandy, France, on Omaha Beach just after D-day. The front line was only two miles away. He remembered there was always return fire, shots being fired back and forth. He was in the middle of a war.

Casey was part of a detached unit of twenty-one men known as the 126th B Company. They were at this time based at Saint Maur, France. He remembered how awful the weather was—snow, rain, and plenty of mud. "Rain, rain, rain, and mud up over your shoes," he said. "You'd get into your bunk at night and it was soaking wet. It was awful." He'd dig the snow out and put up his tent, then put the blanket on the snow or wet mud and sleep. He'd be wet and soaked. They'd take outdoor showers and wash their clothes while showering in the cold.

Casey's primary job with the army was as a welder. He made a much bigger difference than he humbly admitted to. He explained how while in France, "the Germans were putting cables across the roads to catch us as we drove. It was a small cable—you couldn't see it until you were right on it. I wanted something on the front that would catch it and break the cable. I welded on the front bumper a post with a hook. The cable would come up [the post to the hook] and break the cable." He welded angle irons on the jeeps, preventing the decapitation wires from doing their jobs and probably saving thousands of lives in the process. As the supervisor, he made sure they were all done correctly. He further explained that the jeeps had to ride with the windshields down for safety in case they hit a cable. "It would send glass everywhere."

Casey also had three-foot chains mounted on the sides of the tanks, swinging around to explode ground mines before they were stepped on by the troops. There were always troops marching behind and around the tanks. "It wouldn't hurt the tank. It was made to kill you and I."

Another Casey story had him going to a hospital after seriously hurting his elbow from a fall. He was actually in a moving truck and noticed the truck in front of them had boxes of food rations. So while the trucks were moving, Casey crawled to the front of the truck as the driver pulled up close to the food truck. Casey was pulling out cases of food when he slipped and hit his elbow on his own truck. "It hurt like hell. I was all black and blue, my chest and all." After they bandaged him up, he was sent back to his crew. However, he was on his own to find where they were. He spoke a little German. No one would help him when he asked if they knew where the American troops were. He was alone and pretty scared of the journey to find them.

Casey also told a story about working twelve- to fifteen-hour days to modify a tank turret. One evening, he took a break and went to the mess hall for coffee. "While I was there, I heard Bing Crosby singing, 'I'm dreaming of a white Christmas.' I cried like a baby. It was the first time I heard that."

During the invasion from France into Germany, Casey recalled, "We had many of the German soldiers surrendering long before the war ended. They were cold, tired, hungry, and just gave up."

The ride back to the United States was in an Italian ship that was captured and used by the Allies. They had about five thousand men on board. The seas were horrible, and Casey stayed on the top deck with a friend. Everyone else was seasick and vomiting. The smells and sights were terrible, and there was no one to clean it up. When they finally reached Stateside, their green military coats were white from the sea salt from staying on the top deck away from the sick.

John F. Casey received his honorable discharge on December 2, 1945, after forty months in the ETO. Thank you, Mr. Casey, for your long, difficult battles to keep us free.

JOHN F. CASEY

CASEY LEARNING THE MILITARY WAY

JOHN F. CASEY

HIDDEN BUNKERS FROM COLLECTION
OF PHOTO'S, JOHN F CASEY.

Walter Cutting, a Fitchburg, Massachusetts, resident, was trained as a navy medic in San Diego. He had only thirteen weeks of training and was in a graduating class of five thousand. The war ended less than a week after graduation, and Cutting found himself at a US naval hospital in Oakland, California. There, he practiced his training on the returning wounded. However, he and his colleagues were not properly prepared for the horrors they would be encountering. Plane after plane brought in more and more of the badly wounded and maimed. Survivors of the Bataan Death March became his patients as well as various POWs—mostly from the Pacific theater. Cutting enlisted and served for nineteen months and thirteen days. He was not even twenty years old at the time. He witnessed the aftermath of the horrors his fellow soldiers had had to endure overseas as well as the effects on ones who got bad news when they returned. Many of those who were POWs in a war with no certainties saw spouses or girlfriends "move on." They were now also getting news about friends and family members who'd been killed in action. A young medic dealing with traumatic life changes had to numb himself to be effective.

Mr. Cutting, thank you for your patience and understanding during those dark times.

Mario Lanza was a Leominster resident whose parents were born in Italy. He had a twin brother, Ubaldo. Together, they served in the same outfit in northern France, Rhineland, and Central Europe. They were drafted in July 1943, and in August, they boarded the *Queen Mary* headed for Scotland. As Lanza put it, "I went in as a boy and came out a man." He was a soldier with the US Army, Battery A, 132nd AAA Battalion, Seventh then the Ninth Army.

They put out sixteen different guns to fire at enemy aircraft. The batteries could pick up and be moved in half an hour. They had a crew of a hundred men to run everything: five trucks, gun crews, generators for electricity, a kitchen crew, a separate three-quarter ton truck for communications, and much more.

They slept on everything from deep snow to straw mattresses in barns—whatever was needed. Lanza said, "I wasn't a hero, just followed orders," echoing a sentiment from all the rest. They crossed the Rhine River, but not before marksmen shot out all the German mines waiting for them.

They did get to visit Italy, sort of. The boys had a week off and during that time decided to go for a walk. They were close to the Italian border, so they just crossed over. They walked "about five feet into Italy" and could now say they were finally in Italy.

Mr. Lanza, your efforts never went unnoticed. We cannot thank you and your family enough for your sacrifices.

United States Navy

HOSPITAL CORPS SCHOOL

Certificate of Graduation

THIS IS TO CERTIFY, That _____ CUTTING, WALTER HENRY _____

Hospital Apprentice Second Class 531 91 41 V6

a _____ in the United States Navy, having

satisfactorily completed the prescribed course of instruction for the HOSPITAL CORPS, has

this ___19th___ day of ___October___, 19__45__ been awarded this Certificate of Graduation

by the Bureau of Medicine and Surgery, Navy Department, Washington, D. C.

Given at the HOSPITAL CORPS SCHOOL,

San Diego, California

C.R. LANE

Captain

Medical Corps

Commanding Officer

Officer in charge,

№ 118966

**HOSPITAL CORPS SCHOOL CERTIFICATE OF
GRADUATION FOR WALTER CUTTING.**

MARIO LANZA

280

GERMAN RADAR. MARIO LANZA IN THE BUCKET

UBALDO LANZA, "UBALDO NEEDED A HAIRCUT"

Erwin G. Markowitz was born August 21, 1923. He enlisted in the US Army on November 11, 1942—Armistice Day, from World War I. He reported to Fort Devens, Massachusetts, before being transferred to Camp Perry, Ohio. At Camp Perry, five people lived in each little shack with just a coal stove for heat.

Markowitz's life took quite an unexpected turn while he was at Fort Knox, Kentucky. At that time, Markowitz was a corporal with the 449th Company of the 159th Ordnance Battalion. Out of the blue, he was ordered to report to headquarters. HQ told him to report to the medics. He knew nothing about medicine and tried to explain his lack of medical experience. They told him not to worry about it; "you'll find out," they said. They just needed someone to fill a spot in the medical detachment.

Markowitz recalled the first time he had to inject a needle into a patient. "I pulled the syringe out and left the needle sticking out of his arm. He was bleeding a little and looking at me dumbfounded. The others would later make fun of me from that first attempt." Most of the others had gone to medical school. He was the only one who didn't go. But he soon received on-the-job training—amazing.

Markowitz eventually found himself being ferried to the *Queen Mary* to be taken overseas. He remembered (with a smile) the naiveté of a fellow soldier from Kentucky talking with him on the forty-minute ferry ride to the *Queen Mary*. It was a tight ride, with soldiers standing on their duffel bags and shoulder to shoulder. The other soldier asked him in a thick southern drawl, "Ern, are we gonna go to Europe on this thing?" They were still on the Hudson River.

After sailing on the enormous and crowded *Queen Mary* for about five days, they finally disembarked in Scotland. Markowitz was transferred to England to a place called Camp G-25, near Tewksbury. Then, he was off to Southampton. "Things were real bad there," he remembered. By now, it was January 1945, only seven months after

D-day. The Battle of the Bulge was in full swing, and casualties were starting to mount. They were "pulling people for replacements—they came to us," just as they did all the units, and picked soldiers for the front lines.

Markowitz remembered that the ship ride from Southampton to France was also a real mess. It had been one of the worst winters in years, and they hit a terrible storm. Down below were bunks for soldiers to "sleep" on. Below the bunk level were trucks and jeeps. One of the jeeps broke loose and began smashing against the deck below, crashing with every wave and the subsequent pitching of the ship. Between the noise and the pitching, all the passengers were getting sick and vomiting everywhere—on the stairs, on the floor, and on each other. All these young men were off to an unknown war in a foreign land, and the trip was going from bad to worse. At one point, a tarp covering the opening above them filled with water that poured down onto everyone below. They started to scream to each other that the ship was sinking. Markowitz remembered thinking, *Thank God*. It was an awful start. Mother Nature won that battle, and the ship had to turn back for Southampton to try another time. Markowitz's total time in England ended up being only a couple of weeks in December 1945 before crossing the English Channel into France.

Upon finally reaching France, they were constantly moving forward, gaining precious ground. They were in Marcai, France, when they heard the news that the United States had dropped an atomic bomb on Hiroshima, which was followed by a sigh of relief and hope. The troops were all well aware that their next battle—after Germany's eventual surrender—would be with Japan. No one was looking forward to battling an enemy that had sworn to never give up and to fight to the last breath of the last man. Surrendering was not an option for the Japanese armies.

The troops were stationed near Soissons, France, where there was a big railway station. Ammunition and gasoline were stockpiled everywhere. German POWs were working alongside French civilians, loading and unloading the trains. There was talk about the place being sabotaged. It was not uncommon for German POWs to cause as much havoc and confusion as possible when the opportunity presented itself. Sure enough, things started to explode, and everything was catching fire. Markowitz and another medic quickly tried to spring into action, bandaging a few soldiers and caring for others who'd suffered various wounds. But smoke, fire, and noise were everywhere. They couldn't even see. They had to lie down between the tracks just to use the rails as cover. They decided after a while to move away from the mess and find cover while the explosions and smoke continued. They were trying to run but were slowed down, stumbling over things beneath their feet.

Markowitz noticed an entire freight car with its side blown off; all the contents—mines—had been emptied and were covering the area. These particular mines were designed to go off when they were stepped on or driven over. During shipping, a clip was inserted under them so they wouldn't explode when depressed or stacked. Markowitz doesn't know why none of them malfunctioned and went off, as they stepped on them to escape the explosions. At that time, they were stepping so quickly, they were just about flying over them. As a result of that day's explosions, he's had to wear two hearing aids ever since. They also tried to dig a hole for safety, but to no avail. It was all cinder and rocks. "It was wild," he remembered clearly.

From there, he was on to Bayonne along the Moselle River, where he expected to stay for quite some time. It was another ordnance area where they had ammunition to deal with—to stack, store, and ship out. There were many German prisoners there as well to help handle the heavy work. The medics had taken over a house; actually, it was the mayor's chateau. It had wide, long windows overlooking the town's square. He could see the soldiers working and could practice his new trade as needed. "One day, a jeep pulled up," said Markowitz. "I see somebody sitting in the backseat, hunched over. I thought he was black. We had a lot of black troops." It was a person burned all over. His whole face had been "melted down like a mask." They brought him inside. "What can you do for him? His clothes were gone, ya know. He had his hand on his leg; the flesh was just peeled off. The doctor wasn't around at the time, so I told the other medic, 'This man's not going to live.' The sounds coming out of his tiny mouth were unbelievable. I gave him some morphine to kill the pain, but it didn't do him any good. So I kept giving him more and more morphine. I was going to help this guy ..." He paused. "... go away." The other medic with him said the doctor was going to be angry that Markowitz had used up all his morphine. "I said, 'This man is suffering beyond words.' I pumped him full of morphine and finally, it was over." Afterward, they were told he was a German prisoner, but "it didn't make any difference" to Markowitz. "He was a terribly suffering human, and I knew what I had to do." When the doctor returned, they told him what had transpired. The doctor looked at Markowitz with a stern face and said, "Markowitz, you did the right thing."

During his stay in Bayonne, some of the local children had found a small grenade that hadn't been discharged. Of course, they didn't know it was operational, and they were playing with it. The French children were living at a nunnery, and one of the nuns happened to be walking by when it exploded. Markowitz remembered running outside his chateau to take care of them. One little girl's upper leg was badly wounded. He could see the bone sticking out, although it wasn't bleeding badly. The blast must have cauterized the wound or she would have bled to death. Markowitz put sulfur on it, as was the remedy, and bandaged her up. "They took her by truck to a hospital in a nearby town," he said.

One of the other medics noticed a trail of blood in the street. The trail led them to the nunnery; they weren't aware the nun had been hit, but she had been hit in the thigh pretty badly. Of course, they had to pull the nun's habit up to treat her, which may have caused the nun more pain than the wound. Markowitz bandaged her up and then sent her to the hospital. A few days later, they saw both the little girl and the nun. "They saved her life," he said of the little girl. The nun was also fine. However, she embarrassedly thanked them before looking away. The little girl's father was so appreciative that he cooked up a special dinner for the medics and shared some "homemade brew" with them.

Markowitz talked about fishing, a love he had even during the war. Although they went fishing in the Moselle River, he was told to be very careful of German mines. He cautiously went anyhow and smiled when he caught a four-pound mackerel. Markowitz gave it to the owner of the chateau where they were staying for him to prepare the delicacy of fresh fish. The Germans, however, strafed the building while they tried to eat their dinner. Apparently, the Germans mistakenly went after the wrong building. The men just finished their dinner.

Markowitz was honorably discharged in February 1946 after serving his country for thirty-nine months. After returning from the war, he wasn't sure about his future. He decided he did not want to be part of the "52-20 Club"—fifty-two weeks of getting twenty dollars per week, which was offered to returning soldiers at the war's end. He was also tired of taking orders. At first, Markowitz thought he might be better suited as a doctor. Thinking medical school was in his future, he considered how he'd spent the last few years. But it was about that time that his father bought his first few knitting machines. Markowitz decided to work with his father in their own business, and together they opened Red Knit Mills and stayed in the knitting business through good times and hard times.

Markowitz's lifetime passion, however, is photography. He's traveled the world taking incredible photographs of wildlife that have been on exhibit at many galleries. His work can be seen at the Griffin Museum of Photography, the Ward Museum in Maryland, the Fitchburg Art Museum, and other galleries throughout central Massachusetts.

Thank you, Erwin Markowitz, for your courageous service to your fellow soldiers and your country.

ERWIN G. MARKOWITZ

MARKOWITZ DIGGING HIS FOXHOLE.

RUBBLE OF PEOPLE'S LIVES FROM MARKOWITZ'S CAMERA.

MORE INCREDIBLE DESTRUCTION AS MARKOWITZ'S
CAMERA CONTINUES TO CHRONICLE HIS WAR.

A church stands amid more rubble.

Anthony Hmura was born July 3, 1923, in Worcester, Massachusetts. Like many of the veterans and Americans at this time in our history, his parents were immigrants. They came to the United States from Golitzia, Poland, in 1919. His father became crippled as a result of drinking Jamaican ginger when he was only five years old. Anthony was the youngest child of three girls and three boys. He had to find work to help support his family; one side job he created was raising worms for the local fishermen. He cultivated them and sold them to the sportsmen in the area. Quite the entrepreneur, he'd amassed a nest egg of five thousand dollars by the time World War II started in 1941—and he was only eighteen years old.

Hmura graduated from Commerce High School. "People took things in stride—very patriotic," said Hmura of his high school days. "Everyone was purchasing war bonds and stamps to help out the war effort." He remembered, "saving the bacon fat to bring to a market. Saving metal and cans to recycle—everyone participated. Everything was rationed."

Hmura continued, saying, "Everyone was in danger. If we waited one more year, the Germans could have been in America." Hmura's number came up, and in 1943, he was in the US Army Air Force. He served in the Eighth Army 445th Bomb Group, 701st and 703rd Bomb Squadron. Hmura was assigned to Tibenham, England, on a B-24 Liberator as an assistant gunner, top turret gunner, and waist gunner. By the war's end, his twenty-eight flying missions would decorate him with four Air Medals, two Presidential Unit Citations and the ETO (European Theater of Operations) Ribbon with three battle stars.

He checked all the gunnery. "It was so cold, you needed to fire the guns just so they wouldn't freeze." He wore a heated suit and gloves. They had to use oxygen at ten thousand feet and above, using a rebreather oxygen mask. Before the war, Hmura had attended art school, and his drawings of photos on the backs of the bomber jackets for the airmen made him very popular.

The greatest loss of any group in the 8th Air Force was September 27, 1944, above the Werra Valley near Eisenach, Germany: As the result of a six-minute aerial battle, thirty-five 445th Bomb Group B-24 Liberators and 336 men who made up their crews suffered the greatest losses to a single group in a single day in aviation warfare history. Twenty-five of the heavy bombers were downed inside of Germany's borders. Three crash-landed, two in France and one in Belgium. Two made forced landings at an emergency field in England, and another crashed at Old Buckenham, leaving only four to return to base in Tibenham. A total of 117 airmen of the Mighty Eighth's 445th were killed in action, 121 were taken prisoner, and only 98 were returned to duty.[32]

The B-24 crew was Lieutenant Otto "Skipper" S. Tauer, pilot; Lieutenant Bob "Gimper" Conrad, navigator; Lieutenant Phil "Toggle" Goldfarb, copilot; Lieutenant Bob "Livy" Livingstone, navigator; Lieutenant Abner "Mate" Musser, bombardier; Lieutenant Harold L. "Head" Clark, navigator; Sergeant Maurice "Pappa" Guerriero, radio operator; Sergeant Anthony "Casanova" Hmura, top turret gunner; Sergeant "Dutch" Shultz, waist gunner; Sergeant "Bill" Trollinger, tail gunner; and Sergeant Bob "Ike" Eisenberg, engineer.

Hmura and his crew flew in the raid on Kassel. The groups were attacked from behind by 100–150 Luftwaffe fighters. Accounts of that day and those six minutes are very detailed and available at the www.445th.com website: aircraft being shot down, blown up in flames or in pieces; midair collisions; flak; and an awful loss of lives. Returning from the Kassel raid, they had eighteen holes in their plane. Hmura remembered with a solemn look, "Only four planes returned that day."

---

32 Kasselmission.com October 2016.

The German Air Force lost twenty-nine aircraft, and eighteen pilots were killed in action. It was a very bloody and costly six minutes.

"The flak was rough. Every time we came back, we had holes in our plane," Hmura said. While the flak came at them, the crew had silver strips called chaff that the crewmen threw out of the aircraft to confuse the German radar systems. But "the enemy was good and didn't miss often." Thirteen times, they were the lead plane of B-24 Liberators.

One of his officers and friends was Jimmy Stewart—yes, the actor. "He was a regular guy, an operations officer for the 703rd. We had about 130 people. Stewart took about five of his crew in a weapons carrier, and we'd go see Clark Gable. I shoulda got signatures, but thought I'd be dead, shot down, so I didn't bother. I didn't think we'd live, honest." Jimmy Stewart offered to put Hmura in the movies when they returned after the war. Hmura actually went to Hollywood for a month after the war and waited for Stewart to return. Stewart, however, wasn't discharged until 1946, with the rank of brigadier general. While in Hollywood, Hmura met up with Jimmy Cagney and his friend Audie Murphy, World War II's most decorated soldier. Hmura enjoyed plenty of celebrity meetings in the coming years.

They went to London on a pass if the weather was bad and they couldn't fly a mission. "The bombs would be going off and the place was a mess," remembered Hmura. "People just walked around the rubble and got on with their lives."

Hmura recalled how they would sometimes "sleep with double blankets—there was no heat. But we ate pretty good." Hmura was also shot down twice. They glided and bailed out over friendly territory where the French underground helped them. "I was armed with two .45s and gave them to the French for helping," said Hmura, who seems to have taken it all in stride.

Hmura recalled that he had met President John F. Kennedy three times. During one of those visits, President Kennedy called to meet with him. "They kicked everyone out of the room. It was just the two of us, and we talked about all kinds of issues—conspiracy, the Federal Reserve System." The walls of his office are covered with signed photos to him from President Kennedy and many other notable politicians and public figures.

Hmura is very grateful for the life he leads. In 1946, he opened Leader Sign Company in Worcester, Massachusetts—"a complete sign manufacturing and service," he said—and he still operates the business today. For many years, he's been known as the Polish Santa and has handed out more than five thousand dollars a year in fifty-dollar bills to random people during the Christmas season. When asked how we won the war, Hmura answered, "We outnumbered them."

Mr. Hmura, your help keeping our country safe from tyranny has been greatly appreciated.

SERGEANT ANTHONY HMURA

HMURA LOOKING HAPPY TO BE OUT OF HIS LITTLE TURRET.

HMURA KNEELING, SECOND FROM RIGHT

HMURA STANDING SECOND L-R

Raphael Godin was born in Fitchburg, Massachusetts, on June 25, 1925. His parents each came from very large families. His father's side had twenty-one children and his mother's side had fourteen children. Godin had an amazing thirty-three aunts and uncles.

Although Godin's folks lived in Fitchburg, they moved to Burlington, Vermont, when he was six. He remembered that his father was very tough on him as a boy, not providing much encouragement.

In the spring of 1943, Godin went to visit an aunt in Windsor Locks, Connecticut. On his way home, he decided to enlist in the United States Navy. That day was April 3, 1943, and he was not quite seventeen years old. After completing boot camp, Godin was sent to Newport, Rhode Island, for signalman training. There, he had four months of training on how to communicate from ship to ship using signals only: flags, lights, colors, and Morse code. Godin was proud that he could memorize all the flags needed for the ships. He was good at his job and knew it was important.

Godin was on a fleet in the southern Pacific that performed invasions on many of the Japanese-occupied islands. However, as signalman, he never left the ship. He also didn't need to carry a sidearm—although he remembered how they'd have machine-gun practice off the back of the ship.

Godin would be high up on the top of the ship in the conning tower. This area is usually armored and precisely where the captain must be during battle; it's also the site from which everything is basically controlled. Godin sent messages back and forth to the ships. Fifty ships could all get their orders in various ways. The flags all went up, signaling the next move. When they came down, all fifty ships would turn, all in line, an amazing sight.

Godin remembered being up high on the conning tower one time when he spotted a kamikaze coming right at him. The crew below was yelling, "Kamikaze, kamikaze!" Godin jumped down from one deck to the next deck, "because I was so scared. Then I said, 'What am I running for? The guy hits the ship, it's going to go right through it anyway.'" Just as he got onto the main deck, the kamikaze aircraft decided to make a loop around, and crash-landed into a nearby Australian cruiser. "The bombs and torpedoes were all there, just like you see it on TV," he said sadly.

The signalman's shifts were four hours on, eight hours off or four and four, twice a day, every day. The Japanese flew between ships, looking for the transport ships carrying supplies. Those were their real targets. The carriers saw all the action, but were also hit by the ruthless kamikaze. Godin was also trained to be in an LST, or landing ship tank. Godin said they used to call it large stationary target, because it could go only eight knots at top speed. They could hold up to forty tanks, twenty on the top deck and twenty on the bottom deck. Sometimes they mixed it up with other trucks that needed to be delivered.

Godin was transferred to the 740th. His commanding officer there was Commander Hampton. Godin remembered him as "a great and very friendly man." The crew built Hampton a hut on the conning tower so he could sleep and stay out of the weather. Some days, when Godin had watch, he'd see Hampton get up in the morning to a bunk full of water. He'd just laugh and say, "No wonder I'm not going to make it through this war." Godin knew him well because he was with Captain Hampton for four hours at a time during his shifts. "I liked him," recalled Godin. "He was nicer to me than my own father was."

Godin participated in seven D-day landings on Balikpapan. During the Borneo invasion, he was high up on his conning tower. He saw the Japanese running for cover as the ships opened fire. Godin explained that the signalman had the long looking glass and he "could see white puffs of smoke from the gunfire and soldiers diving into their foxholes."

Once a foothold was in place on Leyte, an enormous fleet of firepower was gathered there for an invasion of Japan to the north.

"There was twenty ships five deep, almost hitting each other," said Godin. He saw the LSTs getting blown up as they tried to go ashore, burned, and sank, with an enormous loss of life.

In August, when the atomic bomb was dropped on Japan, Godin was on board at the Leyte Gulf. "They [the war ships] were all fully loaded, and the entire shoreline was destroyed from American and Australian gunfire." They had no knowledge of an atomic bomb at that time. "We wouldn't have known what the words meant." It really didn't mean much to Godin, because they knew only that "a new bomb was dropped on Japan and they were suffering. A few days later they [Japan] surrendered," said Godin.

Godin's ship went by the sites a couple of months after the atomic bomb was dropped. "Everything was just burned out. All you could see was some chimneys as we passed by." By now, they had eleven hundred Japanese POWs on board. "They were free there and didn't want to fight anymore. They had a pretty free rein once they were POWs and surrendered." Godin had no knowledge of the treatment of American POWs during the war. They were told very little about other events, including the surrender of Germany's Third Reich. "War is a terrible thing," he commented. He vividly remembered more details that he preferred to leave unsaid.

After the war ended, Godin returned to Vermont in July 1946. However, he reenlisted two months later for another two years of military service, until 1948. On July 15, 1950, Raphael Godin married Helen Roy in Saint Johnsbury, Vermont. The couple moved to Leominster, Massachusetts. Unlike his parents, the couple raised only four children of their own.

Godin worked for a while at Independent Lock in Fitchburg. He then returned to his studies and obtained his GED to finish his missing high school years. He attended night classes in science for a college degree for another ten years using his GI Bill, which would pay for his education. Godin even attended Fitchburg State College and eventually became a teacher at Leominster High School for close to seventeen years.

Mr. Godin, the citizens of the United States of America thank you for your service.

SIGNALMAN RAPHAEL GODIN

GODIN DOING HIS SIGNALS WITH PRIDE KNOWING
THE IMPORTANCE OF COMMUNICATION.

Frederick L. Cuddy was born December 8, 1923, in Fitchburg, Massachusetts. He has three sisters. Their mother was born in Canada and their dad in Concord, New Hampshire. However, their dad died when the children were young. Subsequently, their mother and a wonderful stepfather raised them.

After the bombing of Pearl Harbor, Cuddy enlisted in the United States Navy in December 1941. He remembered going upstairs in the Fitchburg post office, where the navy had a recruiting office set up. "You signed up there and went to Worcester for your physical. You'd get a telegram to report to the post office. From there to a Springfield navy base, back home, and then to Newport, Rhode Island, to get sworn in." By January 1942, Cuddy was off to basic training for six weeks again in Newport.

As a result of enlisting, versus being drafted, Cuddy went in as an enlisted boatswain's mate on the USS *North Carolina* battleship. As a boatswain's mate, he was in charge of the deck crew, rope and cable splicing, and crane operating, working out of an area called the sandlocker. He would call her his home for the next three and a half years.

Cuddy boarded the USS *North Carolina* in Portsmouth, New Hampshire, headed south through the Panama Canal, and sailed onward to the brutal war in the Pacific. The *North Carolina* saw a lot of battles. "We were causing trouble everywhere we went," Cuddy said, laughing all these years later. They were always on the move, never in one place very long. This was a new warship, and it took part in every major naval operation in the Pacific theater of operations. She earned fifteen battle stars and was the most highly decorated American battleship of World War II. The warship was 730 feet long and could cruise at 28 knots with a range of more than twenty thousand miles. It had a full crew of 2,339 men. The *North Carolina* also had two catapults that would launch the three Vought OS2U Kingfisher floatplanes when needed.

Cuddy explained about the danger of an aircraft having to come back and make an unannounced emergency landing. It was known that American gunners accidentally shot down some of our own planes. "The guys on the guns figured our planes were going out there [and] anyone coming back here has to be the enemy," he said. The other concern was having them crash-land on the deck. "All the other planes are running and all fueled up, he comes in and hits them, and they'll all blow up.

"Going in on an invasion, we had the sixteen-inch guns. You'd put the projectile in and six bags of powder. We would start firing from twelve miles out. Or, if we were going broadside, we'd have three guns going. When they would fire, the ship would just rock back and forth, level off, and fire again. When you get out of range, the next ship would take over and you'd make a turn around and come back up the other way."

On September 15, 1942, a Japanese I-15 torpedo hit the *North Carolina*. It was hit port side, twenty feet below her waterline, and took the lives of six of her men. The torpedo created a hole approximately eighteen by thirty-two feet. She was patched up and returned to Pearl Harbor for more permanent repairs. "When we first got to Pearl Harbor, it was like it was just bombed the day before. They were trying to keep the ships that were mobile, keeping them going, so the other stuff that was sitting on the bottom was still sitting there just as it was [when they were attacked]," explained Cuddy.

Cuddy had known Cecilia Crowley since the mid-1930s. While he was on leave in 1945, the two got reacquainted. On just their second date, Cuddy proposed marriage. She asked him, "Have you been drinking? Come back and ask me another day." So he met up with her the very next day and asked her again; she accepted, and they were married in July 1945.

During Cuddy's last six months in the navy, he worked on tugboats in California. Mrs. Cuddy traveled with him there and found work with the Department of the Army POW Camp in Treasure Island. After the war, the couple moved back to central Massachusetts and settled in Lunenburg. They have a close family of three sons, a daughter, eight grandchildren, and twenty great-grandchildren.

Mr. Cuddy, we cannot thank you enough for your service to this great country you helped protect.

FRED CUDDY, UNITED STATES NAVY

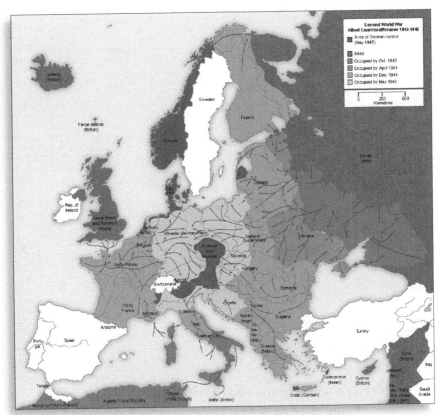

HTTP://WWW.U-S-HISTORY.COM/PAGES/H1709.HTML
COURTESY OF ROB AND ALICIA SPOONER,
OREGON COAST MAGAZINE

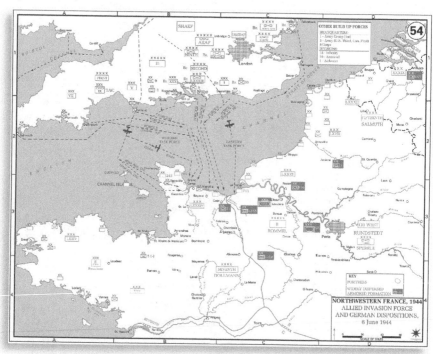

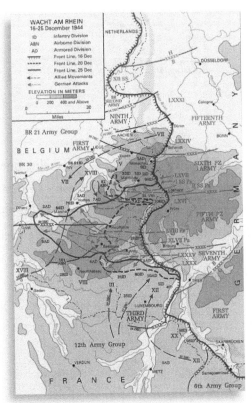

THE BATTLE FRONT LINES AS THEY CHANGED
TO FORM THE BATTLE OF THE BULGE.

VALERA - STANDING

Once again, in this time of history, we are facing uncertainty about our precious American freedom. Although we can never thank those who perished during World War II, nor can we ever really thank the survivors enough for their efforts, we can continue their diligence by protecting each other as they protected us those many years ago. Thank you, America, for getting us through those tumultuous 1,364 days of uncertainty.

In all, the numbers are staggering:

The USSR alone lost 26.6 million lives.

China estimates are as high as 50 million dead.

The United States counted 419,500 lost lives.

Germany lost 8.8 million, Japan 3.2 million, and Italy 457,000. The Axis powers lost 12.5 million lives altogether, and Holocaust victims were estimated at 11 million, including 6 million Jews and another 5 million homosexuals, disabled, and Jehovah's Witnesses.

Estimates are that more than 85 million lives were lost during the largest war in humankind's history. These terrible times were not just old black-and-white film clips from the History channel. They made up the life many of us can say was "my father's war."

FATHER AND SON, AUGUST 1999

CHARLEY VALERA